The Soccer Coach's Blueprint

JASON CARNEY

THE SOCCER COACH'S BLUEPRINT

Build a Strong Team Culture to Create a Winning Environment

Meyer & Meyer Sport

British Library Cataloguing in Publication Data
A catalogue record for this book is available from the British Library

The Soccer Coach's Blueprint
Maidenhead: Meyer & Meyer Sport (UK) Ltd., 2018
ISBN 978-1-78255-143-0

© 2018 by Meyer & Meyer Sport
Aachen, Auckland, Beirut, Dubai, Hägendorf, Hong Kong, Indianapolis, Cairo, Cape Town, Manila, Maidenhead, New Delhi, Singapore, Sydney, Teheran, Vienna

 Member of the World Sports Publishers' Association (WSPA), www.w-s-p-a.org
Printed by: Print Consult, GmbH, Munich, Germany

MIX
Paper from
responsible sources
FSC
www.fsc.org   FSC® C084279

ISBN 978-1-78255-143-0
Email: info@m-m-sports.com
www.m-m-sports.com

CONTENTS

ACKNOWLEDGMENTS

To my wife Tammy. You have made me who I am today. You are the strength and rock of the family. You are the best wife, mother, and friend I could ever wish to have. I love you with all my heart.

To my children, Megan, Emily, Ryan, Quinn, and Ally. I try to be the best I can be. I try to teach you valuable lessons that will help you through life. I am so proud of you all and love you so, so much.

To my two sisters back in Bolton, England. We have gone through some tough times after losing Mum and Dad, but we have come together stronger. I love you both.

To all my ex-teammates. My coaching style has come from you guys. I have learned from every team member that I played with. A lot of credit goes to the Johnson Fold Strollers, a group of players that epitomized team work.

To all the staff at Preston North End FC, especially Gary Peters. You gave me the platform to fall in love with coaching and player development.

A special thanks to everyone at Foothills Soccer Club, Oregon. We implemented a blueprint and watched the players grow. I learned so much and it was great to see a plan come together.

INTRODUCTION

As a child, I loved soccer. I would finish my homework at recess so that when I got home, I could have dinner and then get out on the soccer field. Rain or shine (it was mostly rain) I played with my friends or, if my friends were not playing, I would go out and kick the ball against a wall. I had a great imagination, and when I was kicking the ball against the wall, it was just like I was at Anfield, playing for the mighty Liverpool FC. My soccer imagination was a hindrance when it came to school work. All I ever thought about was the beautiful game. While studying math, English, and science, I was consumed by the thought of playing professional soccer. The time my mind was more at ease was during PE. We always played soccer or ran cross country in our PE classes, so I was way more focused when it was time to exercise.

I grew up in Bolton, Lancashire and became a loyal Bolton Wanderers supporter. My father was a Liverpool fan and was disappointed when I jumped ship to support the Wanderers. I thought it was the right thing to do to help my local team. It became an obsession. I had some great moments supporting the Wanderers. The one that sticks in my mind was the 1995 playoff final that the Wanderers won 4-3. Reading went 1-0 up after four minutes, Nogan with the goal. Williams made it 2- 0 within 12 minutes. Lovell missed a penalty for Reading on 34 minutes, and that was the turning point. Bolton scored a 75th-minute goal to give them hope and, with four minutes to go, De Freitas scored the leveler for the Wanderers. Bolton went 3-2 up in extra time, Paatelainen scored on 105 minutes, and De Freitas scored the Wanderers' fourth goal on 118 minutes. The Reading player-manager Quinn scored a late goal to finish the game 4-3, and ultimately Bolton was promoted to the Premier League. I remember feeling so happy! I was also learning about persistence and teamwork. The Wanderers showed great character that day, and I remember thinking how the coach must be feeling. By this time in 1995, I had already had two opportunities to make a professional team. One was with Bury FC, and the other was with Oldham Athletic, and both times I was unsuccessful. I thought that if I couldn't make it as a professional soccer player, then I wanted to be an expert soccer coach. When I watched soccer games on TV, I always got frustrated when the man of the match was always the guy that scored; he would do nothing all game and then score the winner. I thought the real man of the game was the central defender who tackled well, never lost a header, and barely gave the ball away to the opposition. The next day at work, all my colleagues would be talking about the goal scorer. "Rubbish!" I would now start a debate. "How can someone get man of the match when they only touched the ball twice?"

One of my work colleagues ran a local U11s team in Ramsbottom, Bury, and he asked if I would like to help. I was 25 and thought that even though I was still playing, I wanted to start my coaching career early so that when I finished playing soccer, I would already have about six years of experience as a coach. I had such a great time with the group. I then became a scout for Oldham Athletic. I traveled the northwest of England looking for players that could make the grade as a professional soccer player.

In 1996, I got my big break. Preston North End FC hired me as an academy coach. I was thrown in at the deep end, and I was assigned as head coach of the U16 boys team. I told the club I was not qualified to run the group as I only had my UEFA C license at the time but that I would like to be an assistant. "We don't have anyone else to do it," said the technical director at PNE, "It's all on you."

I thought it was unprofessional for a rookie to be coaching the U16 boys at PNE FC. Not only was I inexperienced, but I was also too young to be given a group of players that only had one year left before a decision would be made about them becoming professional soccer players. I was shocked at the lack of professionalism at the club. That all changed when Gary Peters took over. He was a great mentor for me. I approached him and asked about becoming an assistant coach. He placed me with Ged Starkey, an A license coach who was a good teacher with a great personality. Ged allowed me to have an input and also gave me opportunities to run some practice sessions. After the practices, we would talk about how the practice went, what I did well, and any improvements needed. I look back on those days with fond memories. Gary restructured the staff and the academy. He put together a group of faculty that were humble and authentic. We had one of the most influential youth programs in the northwest of England. After two years with Ged, I was ready to be a head coach. I'll never forget the moment Gary spoke to me about it. He said that I had something that he wished he had: a great connection with people and the players. That was my strength; there is more to coaching than just getting the players to play.

Coaching involves lots of different aspects, and every coach has strengths and weaknesses. I wanted to learn as much as I could about soccer development. I studied the game every single day (and I still do). My obsession to play professionally had now moved to the coaching side.

I wanted more. I was learning a lot, but I felt I needed to understand the game even more. I wanted to travel and experience more cultures. Two opportunities presented themselves: one in New Zealand and one in the United States. In 2003, I headed to the US. I started off in Virginia. In a country where soccer was probably fourth in popularity behind football, baseball, and basketball, I came across lots of players that never really watched soccer on TV. Sure, the kids loved the game; they loved it for that 90 minutes of practice. After practice, though, youth in America have plenty of opportunities to do other things.

Their only improvement would have to come from three hours of practice a week and the game at the weekend. During my time coaching in Virginia, I coached at eight soccer clubs. I had no communication with any of the technical directors of these clubs. They never once came to me with a blueprint for the club. Nothing! In 2008, I moved to Oregon and started working with a local club. After coaching my team for a few months, I asked them about a development plan for their coaching staff.

Their response? "You don't understand soccer in Oregon." It was then that I realized that not many clubs in the US have a development plan—hence the reason for writing this book.

I hope this book will encourage you to create a culture of development and learning. This blueprint will take you on a development journey. I have remembered all my past experiences: I remember some of my old coaches that had no authenticity, I remember the practice sessions being fitness only, boring and unproductive. These thoughts helped me to become a better coach. Young players thrive on having an authentic coach. They crave structure, honesty, and fun. This blueprint works for all ages and levels of ability. We want to keep the most active child occupied. We want players to be at your practice sessions and to tell their parents, "I want to play soccer!"

The system is successful. We define success by development. We should not coach results. We look at performance. This book will improve your coaching style and your players.

CHAPTER 1

THE VISION

The first part of building a culture is your vision. Turn your desire to become a great role model and leader into actions. You need to look at the long-term goal of your club or team. You need to focus on the performances both at practice sessions and at the games. When the environment you are in is committed to learning, then the winning will take care of itself. The vision can start with a mission statement, a statement that emphasizes your beliefs and goals. A mission statement is not merely a description of a soccer club by an external party, but an expression, made by its leaders, of their desires and intentions for the soccer club. The purpose of a mission statement is to focus and direct the organization itself. It communicates primarily to the people who make up the soccer club: its coaching staff and its members. It gives everyone a shared understanding of the club's intended direction. Your mission statement and your playing philosophy are promoted within the club. You should also mention on the club website that you do have a development plan.

You will be able to judge your performance from the players' (and parents') reactions. Players can quietly let you know how they feel about your performance as a coach. If you start with twenty players at practice and in a few weeks it's down to ten, then something is going wrong. There are many other ways to judge how you are performing—don't be too quick to blame the players. More often than not, you are the one who picked the team and now you have to coach them!

I have worked with a few coaches that refused to follow any plan, and I can honestly say that their teams did not improve. The teams stayed in the same low division, and the players did not look like they understood the game. When you do not have a process on development, you will not see improvement.

When implementing a club blueprint, you need loyal, hard-working people by your side. When I sat down with coaches that wanted to join my club, I had an open mind. I took the club blueprint with me and was excited to talk soccer. While I was in conversation with a potential coach, I was thinking:

- Where can this person take me?

- Am I being inspired by listening to this person?

- Is this person capable of encouraging young players to give it their best effort?

- What is their body language when I show them the blueprint?

- How can I inspire them to commit?

- Is this person capable of following the plan and also adding some of their experiences to it?

MISSION STATEMENT

Sample Mission Statement

Our goal is to develop well rounded children who will understand:

- *The game of soccer* – All aspects of the game

- *Teamwork* – Knowledge and awareness

- *Work ethic* – Speed and mobility

- *Discipline* – Courage and bravery

- *How to win* – Technical and tactical awareness

- *How to lose* - Mental toughness

- *Fair play* – Character

- *Enjoyment* – Kids who have fun in soccer try harder, perform better, and stay involved longer

Understanding your mission statement and following through on it are so important when building a team culture. Everyone involved has to share this vision. Your core values have to be included in your statement. You cannot just write something down because it looks good on paper. You have to really believe in what you are doing. As you can see, the above statement does not just include soccer skills, it also involves life skills. You can learn valuable life lessons from sports. Yes, you want to teach the players how to play the game, but you also want them to learn how to treat others and to understand work ethic. If a player is working hard and they feel and see their self-improvement, then the player will be on board with your teaching process. Players thrive on structure and guidelines. If the guidelines are not followed by the coach, then the coach will lose the respect from the players and they will feel cheated.

What does the mission statement mean?

The game of soccer – You are teaching the players excellence. Yes, you allow them to play and learn from their mistakes, but you also have to guide them along. Times have changed. I became a decent soccer player by playing on the streets and with friends. If I had worked with a coach to learn more about the game, I would have been a much better soccer player. Game intelligence is key to building a club culture. Players need to feel like they are improving. If players do not get a sense of self-improvement, they will move to another team or sport. You will not be able to create a team culture if you keep losing players every year.

Teamwork – Picking the best players does not necessarily mean you will have the best team. The All Blacks—the most successful rugby team in the world—have a motto on building a team: "Better people make better players." They recruit players that fit into their team. This is why Sir Alex Ferguson at Manchester United and Bill Belichick at the New England Patriots were (and are) so successful. Their vision of what a team should look like never wavered. If any player disrupted that teamwork, they were kicked off the team, no matter what skill sets they had. This book is similar to that approach. Before you kick a player off the team, try to find out about their background. Communicate with the player and let them know that your job as the coach is to help them. If they continue to work against the team philosophy, then you will have no choice but to let them go. The strength of the team as a whole is the decisive factor in determining the outcome.

Comparing the above professional teams to your team may seem like comparing apples and oranges, but when it comes to teamwork, you should be mimicking the process of the aforementioned teams.

1. How Do You Handle Your Players?

Team building is a product of the coach's credibility. The coach must be honest and must be a good teacher. He or she needs to communicate the vision to the players and have realistic targets while building for the future. For the coach to reach the maximum potential of the team, he or she may need to work on two or three priorities to get the group moving forward.

2. Do You Communicate?

Good communication is a way of perfecting team building; it creates the right atmosphere for players to learn. In your practice sessions, you will communicate the exercise and demonstrate, then watch your players solve the problems.

3. How Do Your Players Get On With Each Other?

There will be a pecking order within the team. The team leader must be one that is respected by all the players. They must also have a close relationship with the coach. Players do not necessarily have to be best friends off the pitch, but it does help. As long as they know their task when they are on the field and in the locker room, your team will be strong.

Work ethic – Once again, the coach sets the standards. The coach is always the first to arrive at practices and games. The players will be more likely to jump on board the development train if they see their coach working hard to make them a better player and a better person. Challenge the players to self-manage. Allow the players to be the disciplinarians of work ethic. Working hard does not guarantee a win; in the coach's eyes it is a win, but not in the players' eyes. You have to educate the players on the importance of work ethic.

I always tell my players, "Be the best you can be today. It may be different than yesterday, but get out there and give it your best effort. Have the mindset of can, will, and do!"

Your practice sessions will be competitive. Every action the players take will have a result. When your practice involves players winning and losing, be sure to watch the reaction of all the players once the exercise is over.

Discipline – Being disciplined does not mean you will not make mistakes. Some coaches equate making mistakes with not trying. This is just not the case. Do not get the two mixed up. No player wants to be punished for making a mistake. Do not punish the whole group if some players decide to disrespect the practice or game. Sit out the players who are not disciplined. Explain why they are sitting out and then ask them, "Are you ready to give it your best?" If a player has good discipline, they will learn quicker and the group will progress at a faster rate. The development process is a lot slower if the coach is wasting valuable time on disciplining players. This should never be the coach's job. This is why, when holding tryouts, it is important to look for the player's attitude first. Ajax use the acronym TIPS—technique, intelligence, personality, and speed—when they are looking to recruit players. The blueprint philosophy uses the same letters, but has them rearranged as SPIT. Many grassroots youth soccer clubs do not get the luxury of recruiting players that have TIPS. If you are a local grassroots soccer club, look for personality as your top criteria. We believe that a player must have a great attitude when embracing the blueprint philosophy. We know that the philosophy of decision making will enhance the player's technique and intelligence.

How to win – Players need to buy into the phrase "Games are won on the practice field." Explain to the players that they need to rely on each other to become successful. It is impossible to achieve your goals alone. As the coach, especially in youth soccer, your motivation is not the win. You must believe in the process you are taking and you must always be looking for excellence. Coach performance, not results but understand that to get the team on board, you need the results. Players want to win; you want them to want to win. Finding that balance as a coach is vital to building a learning culture.

How to lose – The coach (and parents) has a vital role to play when it comes to teams losing. When things are going badly, no one wants to propose solutions because players put their own interests first. There are a thousand excuses when a team loses, but only a few reasons why they lost. Make sure your analysis on why the team lost is accurate and that the players understand. You will come up with a solution to fix it. You cannot turn it into a me-versus-them situation. The message to the team is "We come to practice this week and work on..." When a coach first joins the team, they should discuss dealing with adversity and what they will do if the team starts to go through a bad spell.

For every team I have coached at U13 and above, I use the perfect player table (table 1). I got this idea from Bill Beswick (*Focused For Soccer*) who reshaped my thinking about coaching soccer. I highly recommend that you read Bill's views on sports psychology.

This chart helps me to understand the player's mindset. I look at the answers the players have written down and then I store them away. I only pull them out when a player is having a problem that is related to the perfect player form. I want to see what they wrote. The one that I used the most was the "Making mistakes" part of the chart. I would see players beat themselves up time and time again because, in their eyes, they were not performing. I would sit down with them and show them what they had written on the form at the start of the season. This cleared the air and always seemed to get the player back on the right track.

Table 1 The Perfect Player

Situation	The perfect player responds by...
Dealing with poor form	
Making mistakes	
Poor calls by officials	
Being a goal down	
Being a goal up	
Constructive coaching	
Mistakes by teammates	
The big game	
Being substituted	
Coming on as a substitute	
A run of defeats	
Yelling from the crowd	
An intimidating opponent	

We know that no player is perfect, and I had a few issues with some parents when this form was handed out. You have to explain that this is hypothetical. If the form was called the average player table or the good teammate table, I do not think you would get a true answer from the players. The form is a way of setting standards for themselves and is a great tool to fall back on when the situations mentioned above occur.

Fair play – This does not mean you go onto the field and allow the opposition to mow you over. It means you play with integrity. You do not abuse officials or supporters. Players do not dive or fake injuries to con the referee. Fair play is respected by the team, players, and staff. Your players are able and willing to perform their role within the team.

Enjoyment – Players learn quicker and stay involved in the game longer if they are enjoying themselves. Here *enjoyment* means players being in a learning environment and feeling like they are improving, and being around good teammates and feeling like part of a team. The coach needs to set guidelines and then stick with them. Your practice sessions should be planned, engaging, and fun.

You should never waver from your mission statement. Before joining your team, every player (and parent) should be shown your mission statement and understand that this is about the team.

Here is a summary of how to deal with players at your club or on your team:

1. If a player has no skills and is not willing to work on the aspects of the game, then they would be best taking up another sport.

2. If your player has skills, but they do not listen to you and refuse to use these skills, you will offer support and encouragement. However, you need to see a change in the player's attitude or they will be let go.

3. If you have a low-skilled player who is willing to work at it, you and the club will support that player. You will be patient with the player and you will see the growth in this player.

4. If your players are able and willing, give them responsibilities (e.g., captain). The goal of these players is to move players from situations 2 and 3 to situation 4. Too many good players these days ignore their duty to the team. The job of a good player is to make their teammates better.

With the mission statement in place and presented on your club website, you now need to focus on your coaching staff. You cannot build a teaching and learning culture without your staff. You now must develop a blueprint that can improve your staff—and in turn, your players. Your staff need your full support and, as the leader of the club, you need to practice what you preach. I purposely took the weakest group when I started this plan. In three years, we went from the lowest division at U10 to the premier division at U13. It was sending a message out to the staff that they too can have success if they follow the development plan.

All your coaches will follow the club plan and the club's technical director will constantly monitor their progress. If you do get push back from any of your coaches about the club plan, you need to explain that this is what the club wants and that they are more than welcome to add their coaching experiences to the development plan. If any coach decides to go it alone, then you need to remove them from the club. When I had push back from coaches, I would give them this scenario: If you wanted to play a 4-3-3 and you got push back from one of your players, would you play them?

A successful mindset begins when all members of the staff agree to be led in the same direction. You will inspire and unify the coaches and players and teach them the power of teamwork. You want the staff and players to enjoy the game, be respectful, work hard, be unselfish, and understand the power of being a team. Your players will understand the philosophy: Better people make better players. You want players that play with no fear and understand that there will be road blocks on the road to success. There will be tough times ahead. You embrace these tough times and take the opportunity to learn from them.

You cannot improve without having some disappointments.

PYRAMID OF GROWTH

Team

Self-image is important. Your core values in this pyramid will build your image as a team. All decisions will be made purely for the benefit of the team. Everyone will be held accountable for their actions. To reach your goal, you will work together and do your jobs well. You will encourage each other and stay focused on the task.

Always compete

The only competition that matters is the one that takes place within yourself. Be humble when you win and gracious when you lose. Walk off the field feeling that you gave it everything. Push yourself physically and mentally.

Decision makers and self-belief

Your focus is on continual improvement. There is no fear. You understand that mistakes happen and that you will have poor performances. You do not learn to play soccer because of rules, you learn by making mistakes. Your players are aware of the psychological challenges to building a great team.

Work ethic: Be the best you can be

This is associated with *TEAM*. Champions do extra on and off the field. Always tell yourself, "I am going to be better than yesterday."

Attitude: Better people become better players

A can-do attitude, a positive personality, and a strong work ethic are the foundation of a development plan. Communication between coach and player and player and player will be discussed in a civil manner. You treat everyone with respect.

Your mission statement could now be followed by a playing philosophy, a statement that lets your coaches and players understand your expectations when the game is played. A few questions need to be answered before you implement a playing philosophy, and it would be a good idea to discuss this in a coaches' meeting. Involve the coaching staff so that you get an insight into their thought process. You may be shocked at the amount of opinions you have on a playing style. You will also get the coaches that talk about a good playing style but then go out and preach a different style to their group. A good leader will gather information from their staff and implement the ideas that they think will work.

- Have a staff meeting to discuss the club's playing philosophy. What was your takeaway from that meeting?

- Does the club have the right personnel to follow a playing style?

- Does the technical director allow the coaching staff to play whatever system suits their team?

- Does the club play the same system at U12 and below?

- What is the club philosophy about playing time?

- What is the club philosophy on player positions?

All clubs are at different stages of development and you will have age groups that have different challenges. With all the diversity surrounding your club, you must still follow a core plan. Whatever the skill level of your team, you can still strive for the core values and playing philosophy of the club just as well as the best team in the club. Players react better to structure and guidelines, whatever the level of play.

PLAYING PHILOSOPHY

A controlled-possession game approach with an emphasis on quality passing will be combined with intelligent and timely support and movement leading to penetration up the field to provide goal-scoring opportunities. Because your style of play is based around possession, passing, and control of the ball, it is paramount for your teams to develop the ability to play through the thirds. This can either be on the counterattack or by a patient build-up. So what does this entail? When a team plays through the thirds, it plays from one third to the next (backline to midfield line to forward line) rather than bypassing the midfield. There is no doubt that a pass from the backline into the midfield is a risky proposition that has a chance of being intercepted or stolen. At the youth level, a long ball over the top with a run- and-chase mentality can produce excellent results in terms of winning games. This is why we stick with the long-term development model over a win-now model which is short term.

Even if we know that the majority of our players will never see the light of day at the international level, we must teach all our players in a way that they may have a chance to succeed at the highest level possible.

Defending effectively with all players working to regain possession of the ball will be done aggressively and quickly. Players will have a clear understanding of the tactical objectives of pressure (delay), cover, and balance.

Playing philosophy: Defending

Attitude – Intelligence – Enthusiasm

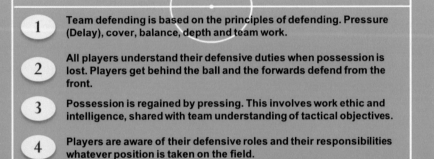

1. Team defending is based on the principles of defending. Pressure (Delay), cover, balance, depth and team work.

2. All players understand their defensive duties when possession is lost. Players get behind the ball and the forwards defend from the front.

3. Possession is regained by pressing. This involves work ethic and intelligence, shared with team understanding of tactical objectives.

4. Players are aware of their defensive roles and their responsibilities whatever position is taken on the field.

5. Players are capable of playing in a flat back four or a back three. Understanding when to mark tight, when to mark loose.

6. All defending is tough but fair and conducted within the laws of the game. Our players relish the 1 v 1 challenge.

Defensive strategy is absolutely essential if you want to attack a lot.

This is a team effort with lots of communication. You teach all your players to defend. Your forwards defend from the front, your midfielders get behind the ball, and your defenders take good positions on the field.

Your team will be taught that when you lose possession of the soccer ball, you press as a team and win the ball back as soon as you can. All players who are potential receivers are guarded at close distance.

Pressing quickly and aggressively will cause the opposition to panic and make mistakes. If opportunities to win the ball back early are denied, players should recover quickly and set up a compact defensive block behind the ball. The team will then force play into areas that will give us an opportunity to win the ball back. In the opposition half, force the ball inside. In the defending half, force the ball wide.

Once the ball is won, you go back to possession mode. Your players will understand they have two different mind sets: in possession and out of possession. The attackers will be focused and move into positions that could spring a counterattack once the ball is won.

- Your players will concentrate and understand the art of defending and be confident in 1v1 situations. They all need to know the defensive stance, when to delay, and when to tackle.

- To be a successful team, you need all 11 players committed to the defensive side of the game. A defender needs to focus, break, and then refocus again as quickly as possible.

- Your training sessions must reflect the same challenges that can occur in a game. Coaching the team on how to defend while out of balance will challenge them to solve problems quickly.

- Because we attack from all angles, players may have to step into another position and cover for one of their teammates who has gone on the attack.

- If your team understands defending, then moving to other formations or playing with 10 players (e.g., if one gets a red card) becomes a lot easier.

- Do you set a line of confrontation when you are winning the game?

Playing philosophy: Attacking

Attitude – Intelligence – Enthusiasm

1. Controlled possession with individual technical and tactical capabilities.

2. The belief that if you have possession of the soccer ball, the opposition cannot score. Trusting that possession will create scoring opportunities.

3. A clear purpose in team play, having the mentality to react to transition of attack or defense. Attack to win games.

4. Be prepared and capable of changing the tempo of the game, counter attacks or slowing down play.

5. Win your 1 v 1 battle. Can your opponent defend? Compete and have intensity.

6. Be capable of adapting to various formations – U9's and U10's 2-3-1 and U11's / 12's 2-4-2, 3-2-3 and U13's up 4-3-3, 3-4-3 or 4-4-2

The greater the control a player has in the final third, the greater the chance you can dictate your style. It is especially important to keep the ball moving and to probe for scoring possibilities. All the players must contribute; from the keeper and the backs to the forwards, everyone has a role to play. The keeper and the backs stay focused when on the attack.

The key to good attacking play is passing angles. Running, passing, and looking in straight lines narrows the view of the game and lacks creativity. It is important to pass short and long and to play angles, not just straight lines. Your players must be able to decide for themselves what play is available by moving into areas that will cause problems for the opposition. Deciding on what kind of pass to make—the accuracy, the weight, and the timing—is now key in creating that scoring opportunity. Players have to understand when to dribble, when to shoot, or when to pass. Playing a passing game does not mean that you will not allow your players to dribble.

Players must see the moment when you can create a numbers-up situation (2v1) or see a 1v1 opportunity with no cover for the defender. If the opposition sees the danger and has sufficient cover, don't dribble. Instead, move the ball with a pass to get away from the compacted area.

The key to your attacking play is the holding midfield players. Whether you play with one or two holding players, the quality of the attacks will be determined by the positioning of the holding midfielder.

COUNTERATTACK

A counterattack is an attack in reply to an attack. Your players will know when the opposition is out of balance once you regain possession. When you see the counterattack is on, the team splits. If they are tightly grouped, you will lose possession quickly. The player winning possession will look to play forward, and others will support them to create more attackers than defenders. The quality of that first pass and movement is key. There must also be a defensive balance to the team. The defensive players move into areas that will prevent a counterattack from the opposition.

THIRD-MAN RUNNING

It is more than just the player with the ball and one player off it; passing must include consideration for the third man. In teaching a player third-man running, pay attention to wide angles and others running into space. When you make wide runs, you open up more room to play into. The art of third-man running is in the speed of execution. With constant practice and repetition, this will become automatic when the game pressure kicks in. An example of a third-man run is when player A passes to player B and player A continues their run. Player B passes to player C who passes to the running player A (see below). Your players will be educated on this kind of movement because it is very difficult for the opposition to defend against and will open up lots of opportunities for the team.

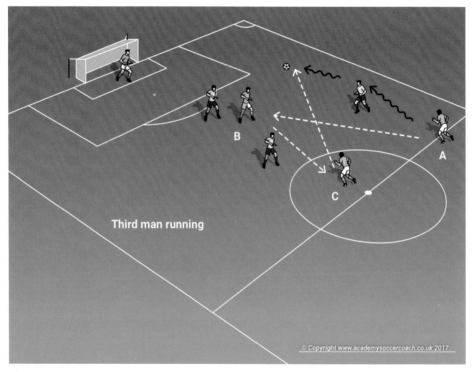

Third-man running

You need a playing philosophy. The vision is to create decision makers and that includes coaching staff. For the system to work, you also need selfless people. People who are open minded and who can discuss your plan in a civil manner. You have to be able to prove that the plan works and then teach it to your staff and players.

In the chaos that surrounds groups of children, we have to make sense of their soccer world. We have to get them to focus and have fun and make them feel like they are achieving something by playing soccer.

Implementing a soccer development plan takes bravery and belief. The philosophy will structure the intelligence needed from your players and coaching staff. You have to focus on the process and not the results of the games. You have to show strength and believe that your development plan will bring long-term success.

DEVELOPMENT

A vision of a player's development

I want my coach to lead me through confusion and uncertainty.

I like to use the phrase, "Water the bamboo." The sports analogy refers to bamboo, a plant which shows almost no growth for the first few years and then grows rapidly, almost overnight. When bamboo is planted, you have to water it regularly and faithfully for three or four years. Years go by in which nothing happens. Finally, after a long time of religious watering, a shoot appears above the ground. The shoot then grows like crazy, often reaching ridiculous heights in just a few weeks. The task is to remain diligent and faithful in your care and watering of the bamboo; any neglect will diminish the growth.

Like the bamboo, this blueprint has a starting point. You have to put all your efforts into your phase I development program. You have to be patient, and you have to believe in the plan.

1. **The first year it sleeps.**

2. **The second year it creeps.**

3. **The third year it leaps.**

Your best coaches need to be running the phase I development program. The leader of this program—with their personality and with the blueprint model—is the foundation of your soccer club. How this leader acts has an enormous impact on players and parents. If you do not get the players engaged at an early age, they will either quit playing and try another sport or they will go and join another club. Selling soccer to the player is the number one priority. It's a proven fact that children that enjoy the game stay involved longer. For the blueprint philosophy to work, you need children to stay involved in the program. Any parent that sees their child having fun and learning will be a big supporter of your program.

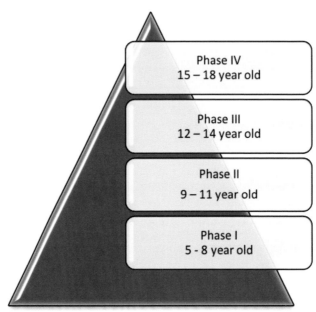

Four phases of development. Note: Your club may not have players as young as phase I. If you are starting your development plan at the phase II group, you can call that phase I.

A vision of a coach's development

The modern coach prepares their players for the modern game.

COACH DEVELOPMENT

- The face of the coach is the mirror image to the team's actions. If you are not positively affecting the behavior of your players, you cannot call yourself a coach.

- Be the expert and the role model. Young players will mimic the actions of their coach.

- Encourage players to be creative. Players must understand that the coach will forgive positive mistakes.

- Be creative when planning a practice session. Do not make your sessions one dimensional. Players will find them boring. Be concerned about your standards as well as your players. Do the right thing for your group not the easy thing. The players need to see that you care and that you are setting the standards when it comes to work ethic.

- Get to your session early and, if possible, set up your whole session. Start your sessions on time. Keep your breaks short (for recovery only), so that players will learn how to refocus quickly and often.

- You are responsible for creating an environment where your players can develop winning habits.

- Understand where you are in terms of club and player level. Continue to strive to be the best you can possibly be.

- Success cannot solely be based on winning games and tournaments. Have a balance between winning and developing a large pool of players that are capable of competing at their highest level possible. If your coaching session is technical and tactical and conducted in the correct manner, then winning soccer games will follow.

- Have rules and guidelines:

  1. We are here to learn.

  2. Be respectful to others.

  3. Become a team player.

  4. Have a great work ethic.

  5. Stay positive.

- Treat all players with respect. If respect is shown by coaches, it is generally given back with effort, concentration, and honesty.

- Work hard and have fun transforming a young athlete's potential into performance. Practices should be fun places to be. Educate your players on the difference between enjoyment and goofing around.

- Focus on potential. Do not just focus on what your players cannot do, focus on what they can do.

- Protect your hard-working players. Do not let the goofballs ruin it. No yelling is needed, just sit them out for a few minutes, then invite them back in by asking them if they are ready to focus.

- Tough love is needed, but do not cross the line.

- Forget about how it's always been done. Become a modern coach. The game has changed a lot, but, perhaps even more so, people have changed, so we have to be forward thinking and be constantly aware of changes within the team. The difficult task is not implementing new ideas but trying to get rid of the old ones.

PARENTS

The team within the team.

A key element in your coaching environment is the influence of parents. The parents are the ones that influence the children to participate, and they need to be made part of your development process. This does not mean they can tell you what formations to play or where their child should be playing on the field. You will get some parents that come and offer unasked-for advice, but you must address the issue with integrity and, if you have followed a structured plan and stuck with the process, you will have a quality answer that they will understand and hopefully agree with.

If the parents see a progression in the development, they will buy into the process and just sit back and enjoy the ride. If you start to look disorganized, stop communicating, and do not give players an opportunity to improve, then the parental support will disappear.

When you think about it, the parent is the foundation of a youth soccer club. The parent is the one who is teaching their child physical, emotional, social, and intellectual development. There will be many times that your team or an individual player will encounter problems. To get the team or player back on track as quickly as possible, you will need a strong parental support. If the parent supports the coach, they will become a huge influence in getting their child back on track.

The one thing players should not be hearing are overcritical parents. If a player is going through a troubled time, then the coach and the parent have to be the supportive structure to help that player get back to enjoying the game. Make it perfectly clear that if a parent has a question or concern, they should talk to the coach. You have to be organized and on top of your communication to the team.

Here are two examples of problems that a coach needs to be aware of:

1. A team has too many subs heading into a game. An email should go out to the parents saying that this week's game will be difficult in terms of playing time because the team has a certain amount of subs this week. Playing time will be fair.

2. Choosing teams. Have a team meeting when discussing the plans for the group. If there is a chance of movement for players, then let the group know there is a possibility that players can move up or down. Emphasize that you will move players up quicker than you would move a player down. Players who do well and show improvement should be rewarded. Players that are struggling need to be encouraged.

These are just two scenarios that would need to be communicated to the team, and there are many more over the course of a season. Parents want to be informed more than ever before because if they are not, some parents use this as an excuse for poor behavior.

Players and parents need to be reminded that failure is part of learning. If you think you can play sports without making mistakes, you are setting yourself up for a perfect storm of emotions and disappointments. Fear of failure is a sure step toward stopping growth. If you fail at something in life, the key is to pick yourself up, learn from it, and move on.

Failure is a part of life and certainly a part of sport. Embracing failure as part of learning something new and knowing what caused you to fail is your feedback. This is why we believe that it's important for players to be good self-evaluators and become students of the game. They have to be able to answer "Why?" and "What?" "*Why* did I succeed? *Why* did I fail? *What* do I need to do to improve?" Failure is critical for an athlete's success. Here is a great quote from Michael Jordan, who was cut from his eighth-grade basketball team:

"I've missed more than 900 shots in my career. I've lost more than 300 games. Twenty-six times I've been trusted to take the game-winning last shot and I missed. I've failed over and over and over again in my life. And that is why I have succeeded!"

The number one criteria when choosing a player to play in the football club is **personality**. This comes from the parent so the parent has to be part of your development structure. **Embrace it!**

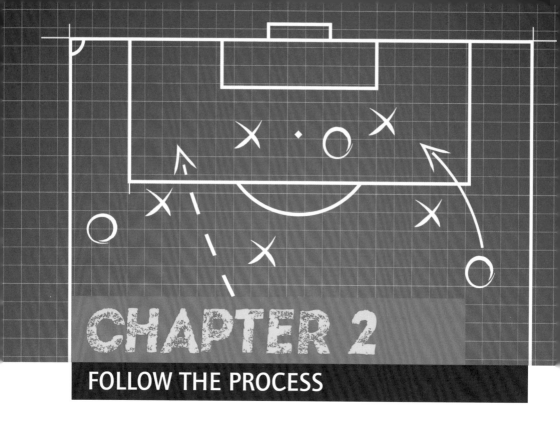

CHAPTER 2
FOLLOW THE PROCESS

THE LEARN FOREVER WAY

Philosophy + Response = Outcome

At your soccer club, you know that the leader sets the tone. The person who implements a development philosophy needs to lead, teach, and inspire the people in the club. It is the job of the leader to develop a vision, set direction, and establish why he or she wants to take the club in this direction. They then need to inspire others to follow the process. The leader must have personality and knowledge of the game. They can step onto the field and prove that the process works. They do not take the best teams in the club just to show they can win. They need to step in and coach teams that are struggling. This is how you prove your process works.

Whether you are a coach or a player, performance follows attitude. With the right attitude, coaches, boys, and girls will commit to the hard work, preparation, and challenge of doing their team job well. They will be encouraged to come out of their comfort zone and understand that soccer is about decision making and working together as a team.

Attitude is shaped largely by

- the personality of the player,
- the influence of parents, role models, and friends, and
- the practice and coaching situation.

Add these three together to get your coaching environment.

Your goal is to give the coaching staff a culture of teaching, developing, standards, discipline, care and concern. This will lead to inspiration for and commitment to the pursuit of a stable soccer program.

The club has to stick to some core principles.

You can add more core values to the above diagram. An additional core value I had was that no player got cut from the team (unless it was due to poor behavior or toxic parents). My team was U10 and I knew the squad would have to grow as we moved from 7v7 to 9v9 and then to 11v11, so there would be room if quality people came along. Players also pull out of your squad for various reasons. At the community grassroots level, I do not believe in cutting young players from a soccer club.

THE BIG PICTURE

Your club will focus all its attention on the player. You want to develop good players and good people. Decisions are made that are beneficial to the player and to the team. You will not succumb to the short-term pressures of winning or feeding coaches' or parents' egos. This is not easy, and it comes with many challenges. You have to be focused on the long-term goal.

What you focus on is:

1. **Coaching excellence, not results**. Constantly teach the process. Do not get carried away with the result of the game. If you focus on results, you will stop doing the things that help to develop a player. If you focus on performance, then you will always be able to work out why you won or lost. Stay in control and the players will also. Judge yourself on the progression of the players and the team, not your win-loss record. Sure, it's nice to win for the sake of the players, but this should not be your motivation.

2. **Being patient.** Teaching the game excellently and ignoring the score does not mean you will not win. You will win more often if you are patient and stick to the process.

3. **Teaching the parents.** Parents will not buy into the process if they do not understand how it benefits their child. Sell the benefits. Seeing their child improve and seeing the enjoyment that they are having will sell the process. Keep parents up to date with what is going on (e.g., practice, game times, etc.). Great communication will help you in the future.

4. **Coaching appropriately.** The process is like a jigsaw puzzle, with each and every one of us responsible for a piece of the puzzle. Be an expert on your part of the puzzle. Work out the top three priorities of the group and also work on each individual player. Inspire the players to keep on improving. **Juggling and long running exercises are excluded from practice sessions.**

5. **Understanding growth stages.** Boys and girls develop physically, mentally, and emotionally at different rates. We have to understand this and not give up on the late bloomers.

6. **Focusing on discipline and work ethic.** The good kids on your team—the ones that come to practice and give 100%—will want you to address the players that give 50% or the players that goof around. These are your values. All your players give 100%. These values do not guarantee you a win; instead, they give each player individual toughness and bind teams together as a unit. Tough love will be needed, but you must not cross the line when discipline is required.

7. **Challenging the players to manage themselves.** Players must be motivated to work on their skills and fitness away from the practice field. Hold them accountable for their actions.

8. **Loving the artist.** Most of your players will become disciplined. They will be good at learning from your coaching sessions. You will get a few players that will create their own patterns of play. This is higher risk but a higher reward. Are you big enough to forgive them for their mistakes? As long as the player is respectful and follows the rules of becoming a team player, then every team needs an artist of some sort.

9. **Remembering the importance of trial and error.** Your practice sessions are challenging. This will lead to mistakes. Dealing with mistakes is the biggest part of player and coach development. It's what happens after the mistake that is important. Learn and move on. Do not be afraid to ask for advice.

DEALING WITH DISRUPTIVE BEHAVIOR

We have all been there. Practice has barely started and already players are out of control. Players are not listening and are staring into space. You have already demonstrated the exercise and now you have to do it again! The players with good attitudes are ready to go, but they have to wait for the coach to deal with the disruptive behavior. Teach players about expectations and that poor behavior is unacceptable. I know there will be other factors that hinder your practice sessions (e.g., bad weather or poor fields), but this is based purely on the behavior of your players. This is the foundation of the blueprint. *What types of disturbances do we deal with?*

Players are late for practice or games

The majority of your players are driven to practices by their parents so when they are late, it's not necessarily their fault. What we can teach them are manners. Every player that is late should walk up to the coach and apologize for being late. They can also say sorry to their teammates. They will gain respect for taking responsibility. If the coach does not receive an apology, the coach should call the player over and ask if they have anything to say (i.e., guided discovery) and search for an apology. When players are late for games, they should never start the game unless the player has communicated the reason for being late to the coach. The coach can now make a decision on whether or not the player should start. Obviously, if you have 10 players and your 11th player is late, you don't have to start them, but you likely would.

I remember a time when I was coaching in Virginia, USA. I was repeatedly telling parents to please get their child to the field on time. After being ignored a couple of times, I needed to take action. At one game, I had seven players at the start of the warm-up and I started with those seven players, even though I had nine players on the bench at the beginning of the game. I played the whole first half with those seven players. I got my point across.

You have to show your loyal players that this type of behavior will not be tolerated, no matter the ability of the player. If you have rules and guidelines, stick to them and the players and parents will follow. We are teaching an important life lesson to the player.

Players are not listening or are goofing around at practice sessions

Remember that you are the coach, not their buddy. Some people have the ability to horse around and still inspire unconditional respect from their players. Some do not. If you are in the latter category, it is important to have respect first. Be respectful and warm but firm. Do not tolerate rude or disrespectful behavior. These disturbances can interfere with your practice objectives. Your players will see this happening. Your loyal, well-behaved players will want you to deal with this type of behavior. Gone are the days of the players being the disciplinarians.

Gone are the days of punishing the group by running or doing push-ups. I have seen coaches stand with the disruptive player and punish the rest of the group. The group is running while the disruptive player watches. This creates anger toward the disruptive player and does not solve the problem. We recommend that you go directly to the source of the bad behavior and deal with it by removing that player from the practice session. Pull the player (or players) to the side and tell them you are not going to put up with disruptive behavior.

I always tell them, "Let me know when you are ready to come back and give it your best." A majority of the time the player will say straight away, "I'm ready," so I let them back in. If not, I leave it for about 30 seconds to a minute and then go over and ask them again. Hopefully, they will then say yes so I can let them back on the field. You could also not start them on game day. Just let them know that, until their behavior improves at practice, they are not going to start a game. I would also let the parents know about this problem. By speaking to the parents, you will be able to get an insight into the child's life. The player may not have a role model. The parents may have issues themselves. By speaking to the parents, you can get a good understanding of why the player is behaving this way.

We need to become the role model by using tough love but also by rewarding them if their behavior does improve. Tough love is needed, but do not cross the line. Be sure to judge each situation in a new light. Some players don't mean to be rude—they just weren't paying attention at the time. Only punish consciously rude behavior. Be aware that some medical conditions can cause children to behave in seemingly disruptive ways. Find out all you need to know about all of your players. There is usually a social issue to why your players are behaving badly.

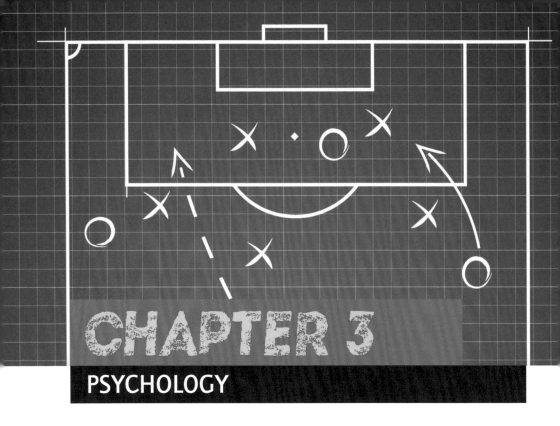

CHAPTER 3

PSYCHOLOGY

BUILDING RESILIENCE

We cannot guarantee many things but there is one thing we can all agree on: We are going to make mistakes. All you ask is for the players to get up every day and be the best they can be on that particular day.

Any game is winnable or losable; the bounce of the ball, injuries, and even a bad call by the official can influence the outcome. The ability to absorb adversity and bounce back is a mental skill that all your players will learn to accept. Some will be stronger than others, but your players know that in times of difficulty they will have the full support of the team. Teams can quickly move from a fighter mentality when winning to a victim mentality when losing. Moments of adversity can be discussed individually or as a team and used as a teaching moment. You will find a solution to the problem by thinking clearly and calmly, knowing that adversity is part of the challenge of being on a team. Finding the solutions to adversity is an exciting challenge. When adversity occurs, you will go back to the blueprint philosophy. You will come across game situations that make you feel like you've been hit by a train (e.g., when you don't perform well or you are expected to win and don't).

Here is how you can deal with these situations.

- **Be calm.** Avoid any emotional overreaction. Accept that these moments happen to all teams. You are no different.

- **Establish the context.** Confirm exactly what the situation is. Help coaching staff and players to rise above the immediate situation and see the bigger picture. You will look for positive points and nail down the key problems and barriers to performance. You will separate the controllable and uncontrollable. You will not make excuses or blame anyone. You will take ownership of your actions.

- **Increase communication.** You will not make this a big deal, but you will increase communication. You will attempt to reduce anxiety and emotion by talking about the process in becoming a good athlete and a good person.

- **Go over team goals.** Go over the philosophy and ask the questions: What has happened? What worked? What didn't work? Who worked? Who didn't work? How are changes to be made (if any)? You will build realistic optimism by coming up with ways to refocus on the process.

- **Be brave.** Tough times don't last, but tough players do. Making changes in the face of adversity can take time and sometimes it's two steps forward and one step back. The group will stick to the agreed-upon plan and continue to support each other. The plan will be monitored to see whether or not it is working.

The coach must communicate the right message with an honest appraisal indicating accountability without blame and identifying what lessons can be learned. The most important part of a player's development is how they deal with adversity. This must be accepted as part of the journey to becoming a winner.

- Get turned on by difficulty.
- Get psyched up by problems.
- Get excited by obstacles.

The six essential mental skills for your players

Confidence—*This is how you make them feel.*

A confident player:

- Is not afraid of having the ball.
- Has a greater chance of fulfilling their potential.
- Maintains positive body language, even after mistakes.
- Will try something different and enjoy being coached.

Commitment—*This describes their motivation.*

This player:

- Is consistent with effort and behavior.
- Feels a sense of achievement from learning new skills and mastering tasks.
- Believes in the process.
- Takes on difficult challenges.
- Encourages teammates.

Control—*This is how well they control their emotions.*

A player with excellent control:

- Feels engaged with energy before practice or games.
- Keeps calm under pressure. Their teammates rely on the attitude of this player.
- Recovers quickly from mistakes and moves on quickly to the next task.
- Does not dwell on disappointing performances.

Concentration—*This is their ability to focus on the right things at the right time.*

This player:

- This player is not easily distracted from their role on the team.
- Stays focused on what is going on around them.
- Knows that mistakes will happen. They have to move on to the next part of the task.
- Is capable of concentrating on their own job as well as their teammates'.

Communication—*This is how they communicate with coaches and talk to teammates.*

This player:

- Encourages and motivates their teammates.
- Listens to coaches' and teammates' instructions.
- Shows respect to everyone around them.
- Can communicate the coaches' instructions clearly to the team.

Courage—*This is how they encourage bravery.*

A courageous player:

- Takes ownership of doing their job well.
- Wants the ball when the game is on the line.
- Plays the ball through the thirds.
- Trusts their team and encourages bravery.

FOCUSED FOR PLAYING SOCCER

Your goal is to excite, engage, enthuse, and capture the energy and knowledge of your players, and channel that toward your vision. You will all agree to the same goals and share the same vision. A strong team bond will help your players become the best they can be.

- We choose the best eleven, not the eleven best.
- We support the vision.
- We think "we" before "me."
- We are mentally ready.
- We are physically ready.
- We are technically ready.
- We are tactically ready.
- We encourage and support each other.
- We take responsibility for our roles.

Success on the soccer field is based on a foundation of player and team confidence. Having the team really believe that challenges can be overcome is a vital part of the philosophy. The journey to becoming the complete player begins by building confidence and then learning to maintain it after setbacks. Learning the game and this philosophy is a challenge not a problem. You embrace the opportunity you have and get excited knowing that every other team member is following the same plan. You encourage your players to ignore the moaners and drive the program with positive energy and self-control. Self-control is one of the most important mental skills in soccer. A loss of self-control will disrupt all aspects of your play and the player may have to be taken from the field. You hope there will be no surprises on the field and that all aspects of your play will be covered on the practice field. Practice sessions will be related to the game, challenging, and fun.

BE THE MOTIVATOR

I once asked a mentor of mine, "How do you know if a young player needs encouragement?" His response: "If they are breathing."

Everyone needs encouragement. Even professional athletes get inspired by positive communicators. Players can quickly lose confidence if their coach is not supportive of them. Positive leaders are great encouragers and it's something the soccer world needs more of. With so many people telling us we can't succeed, we need to hear people telling us we can. Having worked on this development philosophy for the last five years I have seen the impact I have had on young players. Seeing players that know nothing about the game and that lack the intelligence needed to play the game work hard and then in a few years' time, find themselves starting on the "A team."

I remember the doubters when I was visiting the US. "You are going to struggle coaching in the USA." I almost didn't come, but a few days later I spoke with my dad, a man who thought he could do anything and everything. He said, "You go out there. See how they do it. You cannot miss this opportunity." His words made all the difference. For my coaching education, it was the best move for me.

Be the coach you wanted when you were a young player. Put yourself in the players' shoes. What would you want your coach to be like? The world needs more people to speak into the hearts of others and say, "I believe in you. If you have the desire then you also have the power to make it happen. Keep working hard. You're improving and getting better. Keep it up. Life is tough and things do not get handed to you. You have to work on it all the time. Even if you fail, it will lead to something even better. You're learning and growing."

We all love working for and with people who bring out the best in us. We love being around people who lift us up and make us feel great. And while we'll always remember the negative people who told us we couldn't accomplish something, we will always cherish and hold a special place in our heart for those who encouraged us.

So often the difference between success and failure is belief, and so often that belief is instilled in us by someone who encouraged us.

Leadership is a transfer of belief.

Today, decide to be that person who instills a positive belief in someone who needs to hear your encouraging words. Lift someone up who is feeling down. Fuel your team with your positive energy. Rally others to focus on what is possible rather than what seems impossible. Share encouragement. It will help build your relationships.

Here is a text I received from the mom of a player I coached in 2009-2010. I had not seen the family for seven years, and the text was received in 2017.

"I thought you would like to know that as of yesterday, _____ committed to Notre Dame to play soccer. Thank you for giving her such a strong foundation."

I had no idea I had an impact on this player. The impact you have on your players is so powerful. I understand there can be frustrations along the way, but when we say to the players "Be the best you can be," this also applies to the coaching staff.

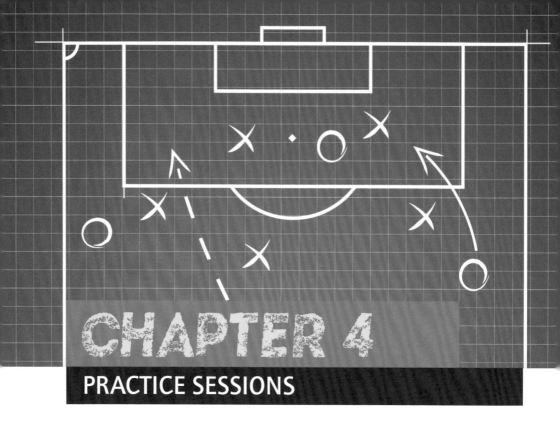

CHAPTER 4

PRACTICE SESSIONS

Take your players where they cannot take themselves.

You will have players that vary in height, size, ability, behavior, and work ethic. To establish a culture of learning, your best coaches need to be with the young players. Lots of good coaches shy away from coaching players that are between the ages of 6 and 10. This is the foundation of your club and where the development process begins. This program needs to have coaching staff that fully believe in the journey of your club. You want coaching staff that are realistic about what this level of player is capable of achieving. You are looking at the long-term plan and where you see these players in three or four years' time. To get the players to grasp an understanding of soccer, there are a few things that you need to conquer.

The overall goal is to conduct practice sessions with enthusiasm that keeps the players engaged. Once the practice is over, the players feel like they have achieved something. The top priorities for the coaching staff to work on with the players in your phase I and II programs are

1. behavior,

2. work ethic,

3. technique, and

4. learning.

If you do not instill the first and second points, then you cannot achieve the third and fourth points. If you cannot get these points across to the players, then you certainly cannot achieve the overall goal.

You have to try and convince your top coaches to coach these young players. If the coach is not excited to be there, then it will not work. The players will get the sense that the coach does not like them, and you will not be able to get the best out of the players. Long-term planning is the goal at this phase of development. Some people will buy into this and others will need convincing. The best way to convince the doubters is to make sure the players are enjoying the game.

Planning your practices is vital. The coach needs to assess the group of players they are coaching and choose the top two or three priorities for the group. What needs to be done in terms of development? This could include things like behavior, work ethic, and technique. At the early stages of development, you should not move away from the three mentioned. A very small tactical part is implemented in practice sessions when the team is playing a game or on game day. Keep it simple.

You need to plan your practices and arrive early to set up. The practice sessions are usually short and you follow these three steps:

1. Phase 1 consists of a fun warm-up while you are waiting for players to arrive.

2. Phase 2 is a technical exercise.

3. Phase 3 is a scrimmage or a conditioned game with certain rules (e.g., small- sided games).

THE PRACTICE BLUEPRINT

- The objective of the practice session is to teach game intelligence.

- Practice sessions should be fun. You provide the foundations that constitute a learning basis from which players construct and develop playing skills and game intelligence (e.g., decision making). Your players will learn, compete, grow, work hard, and feel like they are achieving something.

- Establish a clear philosophy. Work from the end backwards. Your end goal is to produce quality soccer players and people. Let the players know what you are all working toward (i.e., the big picture).

- The practice sessions must include technical, tactical, physical, mental, and social aspects.

- The topic of the practice session must be relayed to the players through planning and organization. Communication is key when coaching. Your relationship with your players is of utmost importance.

- If you have planned your session properly and you know your players, you should be able to work out what level of practice session to run. Have high standards whatever the level. The more the players are aware of your standards, the more realistic they are to achieve and you will be able to hold players accountable for their actions.

- The object of the game is to score so it will help the players if your practices involve scorekeeping of some kind whenever possible.

- Your players need an excellent demonstration of how the exercises work. Do not get frustrated or shy away from practice sessions just because you don't want to demonstrate.

- Cover the coaching points. Have a variation or progression to the practice session if applicable.

- Your club should invest in softer balls if you would like to work on heading. U11s and below *do not* head soccer balls that are the standard size and weight at your heading practices.

- The practice sessions must reflect the game. Have varied practices so that players can see themselves in as many game situations as possible. You should expect your players to have at least 600 quality touches of the ball per practice session.

- Ball-technique exercises should provide plenty of physical activity. A few motivational running competitions and agility training are sufficient.

- Have your players show up to your practices excited and on time. If you challenge them every session, this will generate excitement. They will be less enthused if you do the same thing every week. Your sessions will make them think and move constantly, and the physical demands will mean that when they get a water break, they will use it exactly for that.

- When coaching, focus on the technical and tactical details because the player must understand both. You want players receiving the ball correctly. Players must understand where they pass the ball and how they receive it. Also focus on the players' reactions after they make mistakes. How can you improve their reaction? Players need to know they have your support. Help them through the mistakes.

- You will never master the art of coaching. You have to stay ahead of the game. Becoming obsessed with improving the performance of yourself and your players is a good thing. Success has always been driven by hard work. Coaching is not easy but it helps if you follow a process. A coach who is focused on the process believes that the game is won on the practice field rather than on game day. You will spend more time planning practice sessions than coaching them which does not mean that you are incapable but that you care.

If you focus on results, things will not change. Focus on change and you will get results.

Technique

The natural starting point in the development of a player is getting the body into a good position to receive the ball. Choosing the proper body part to receive the ball, being strong and balanced on your feet, and then applying the proper touch on the ball are all essential to building a solid foundation of good technique. Instruct your players to receive the ball on the half- turn as this will give the players many more options. Receiving the ball using the back foot requires the player to have the correct body shape. This will help the player move the ball more comfortably and quickly. When time and space come at a premium, players with better technique will have more time on the ball and be more successful when using the ball. An absolute priority is to develop a clean first touch. Receiving and positioning the ball as it arrives allows more time to release the ball with an accurate well-timed and well-paced pass. The first touch is the key to becoming a quality player. A good first touch allows you to keep the ball or to play it off the first time, creating a serious problem for the defender. Good technique can find an answer to a game situation more quickly.

Learning environment

I believe in the people, product, and process business model. If you feel you have the right players and you feel you can give them the practice sessions to learn, then players love following a process.

There is really one very simple rule to follow in the development philosophy: Be the best you can be on that particular day. This includes effort, behavior, respect, being coachable, and inspiring others. The learning environment will create a winning mentality. The most important part of this blueprint is based on what happens on the practice field. Every practice session must have a purpose and the players have to be challenged both mentally and physically. No matter how good your session plans are, without enthusiasm, energy, and focus, they will not have the maximum effect.

Coaching styles

- *Command:* "I want you to do this..."

- *Q & A*: "How can you get the ball to the open wide player?"

- *Observation*: "Watch how Johnny opens up his body when receiving the ball."

- *Guided discovery*: "Show me how you can switch the play."

- *Trial and error:* "Recognize the moment to drop the ball back."

Transition

This is the process of going from defense to offense or from offense to defense. Your players should understand both sides to a transition. Young players have a natural instinct to work harder when in possession of the ball. Some do not seem to work as hard when possession is lost. We have to work on transitions at practice so that our players work just as hard at defending as they do attacking. Teaching the players the tactical understanding of transition is so important. Some players will understand it more than others. Know who those players are and get them to be your eyes on the field.

ATTACKING IN TRANSITION

- Your team must be organized defensively before winning possession.

- The first pass must be a quality one that puts the opposition under pressure.

- It is a young player's natural instinct to go directly for the goal. This can lead to the ball being forced into areas that will break down your attack. Players must be quick in transition, but they must also be smart.

- Players must move off the ball into open space and offer support to the player in possession. If they do not receive the first pass, they must constantly move to support the transition. They may not even touch the ball, but their support can still help the transition by taking a defensive player away from goal.

- Our fullbacks attack on the wings. If the team understands this, then the fullback is an easy option for the player in possession.

- You may have an "artist" on the team. Every team needs a player that causes the opposition problems. This can actually help you defensively. One or two more players from the opposition may be reluctant to attack because they are more concerned about the artist.

DEFENDING IN TRANSITION

- Get players behind the ball as quickly as possible.

- How does the player or team react once the ball is lost?

- As soon as possession is lost, the closest player puts pressure on the ball to keep the opposition from playing the ball forward.

- Play with a holding midfield player (or two). This player is constantly in support of the ball being played backwards when you are in possession. Once you lose the ball, they may be the first line of defense.

Transitions must be a part of your practice sessions.

The opposition will be worried about you if your team has good transition skills. They may be reluctant to push numbers forward which will put less pressure on your defenders. You will also frustrate the opposition if you have great defensive transition.

Pressing

Your teams will be taught that when you lose possession of the soccer ball, you press as a team and win the ball back as soon as you can. Pressing quickly and aggressively will cause the opposition to panic and make mistakes. Once the ball is won, you go back to possession mode. Your players will understand they have two different mindsets: in possession and out of possession.

Playing out from the back

At U11 and below, in some countries, the goalkeeper cannot punt the ball. This will force the coach to teach playing out from the back. Goalkeepers are encouraged to play the ball out from the back, but you need to practice this tactical aspect. Do not expect the players to perform this on game day without sufficient practice. Players on the field have to quickly move into open space for this to happen. If this does not happen, then the goalkeeper's options of playing out the ball become less. It takes a lot of courage to do this, especially at the early stages of development. At the older age groups, if there is not an option for the goalkeeper to throw it out, then a punt will be the correct choice. At U11, the ball has to be placed on the ground without a challenge from the opposition and kicked. Players will also be encouraged to use the goalkeeper when keeping possession.

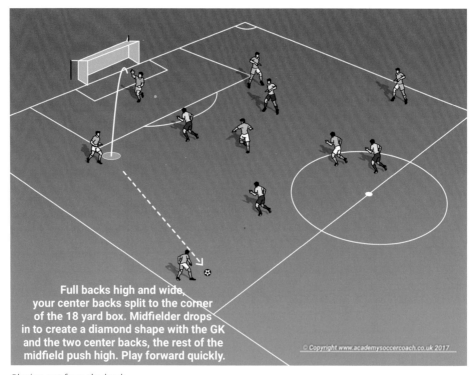

Full backs high and wide, your center backs split to the corner of the 18 yard box. Midfielder drops in to create a diamond shape with the GK and the two center backs, the rest of the midfield push high. Play forward quickly.

© Copyright www.academysoccercoach.co.uk 2017

Playing out from the back

- When the goalkeeper has the ball, the right and left fullbacks push high and wide to force the opposing wide players backwards.

- The two center backs split to the corner of the 18-yard box to increase the distance between themselves and the opposing striker. If there are two strikers, the center backs go wider to create space for the midfield player to collect the ball. If the opposition has one striker, then the midfield can push high.

- The goalkeeper must be heavily involved in this process and must be comfortable with the ball at their feet.

- Once the ball gets played out, can you pass the ball forward? Can your players create an overload? Your players should always want the ball. Playing this way will lead to mistakes, but eventually the positives will outweigh the negatives. Your players will know how to play and not be afraid. We have to encourage them to be brave.

- We still need good decision making from the goalkeeper. If the goalkeeper is not playing the ball out from the back, why? Are they afraid or is no one being brave enough to receive it?

Set pieces

Encourage the players to be creative. Work on corner kicks, restarts, and so on. Both offensive work and defensive work should be practiced. Does your goalkeeper know how to set up the wall? Who goes in the wall? If you have two teams at your practice session, have a full-size game at the end of practice and organize set piece routines. If you are not getting any opportunities to coach set pieces in the game, randomly announce a corner for one of the teams. See how the players react. Teach them.

Defending against corner kicks

At the younger ages, when a player crosses a great ball on a corner kick, it more often goes out for a throw-in on the opposite side of the field. Very rarely will a player get in there in time to put their head on the ball. How do we teach defending against set pieces—especially corner kicks—if players won't head the ball? In some countries, young players are banned from heading the ball. What we have to do is place the players in positions that are going to eliminate the chance of the opposition scoring. Figure 1 shows how the defending team positions themselves on corners. The three key areas are zone marking and all others are man marking. Always leave a striker (4) or two up the field. If you bring everyone back, the opposition will have more attackers.

Figure 1

Position 1: The defender comes off the post—but not too far—to stop any balls being delivered into the near-post area.

Position 2: The defender covers the back post by standing inside the post on the goal line about one yard from the post.

Position 3: This defender stops any low balls that are coming into the danger zone.

Position 4: When the ball is delivered and the attacker can see a teammate is ready to clear the ball, they should quickly move out wide. It is easier for the defender to direct the ball to position 4 when the corner is delivered.

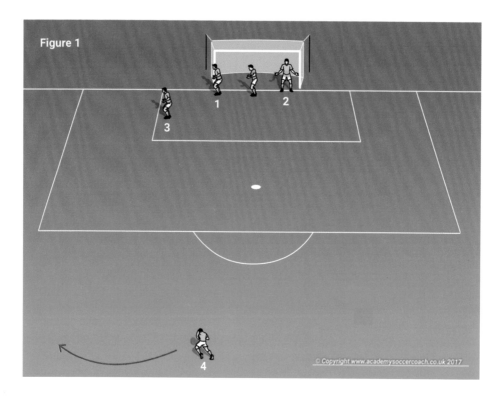

Figure 1

Figure 2

When the corner is delivered to a dangerous area, player 1 now moves inside the goal like player 2. With the goalkeeper and players 1 and 2 now in the correct areas, it gives the opposition a smaller window to score. There will be a lot of swipes at the ball and players ducking out of the way. Having the goal covered is crucial. Player 3 also moves to an area that covers the goal. Player 4 is ready for the clearance.

Have your more tenacious players in position 3 and in the danger zone (6-yard area). Players in positions 1 and 2 do not need to be your best headers or more aggressive players, but they should have some soccer intelligence or quickness. The likelihood of your younger goalkeepers coming out and catching the ball are slim. What they can offer is good communication like "away" or "push out."

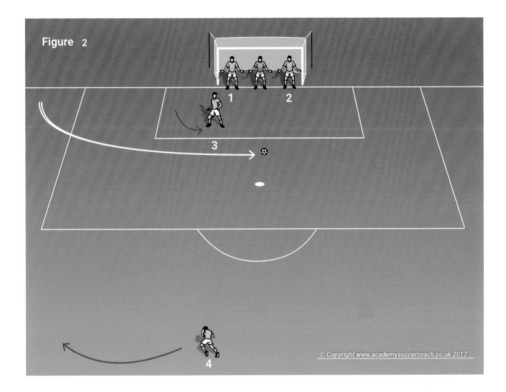

Throw-ins

Ideally, all throw-ins will be thrown to feet. Once a player receives it, the ball will either be played back to the thrower or the thrower will give the instruction for the receiving player to turn. Throws are very hard to defend against if executed properly. The key is quick movement away from the defender and a quality throw to the feet with a quality touch being performed. The thrower must attempt to throw the ball to the receiving player's foot without the ball bouncing. If the receiving player is a good distance away, then the ball can hit the ground first.

Options 1 and 2 show positions on the field where the ball is being passed back to the thrower.

Option 3 shows the ball being thrown backwards and the team switching play from the throw.

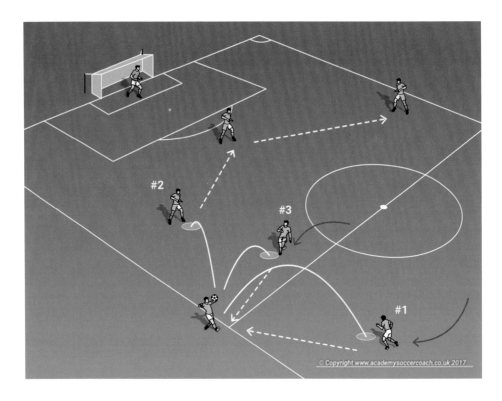

Physical demands

Fitness has to be part of your practice planning. Whether you do your fitness with a ball or without, the goal is to get the player conditioned for playing soccer. Fitness at home must also be part of the player's training plan. Soccer fitness at home can consist of jogging for miles, followed by stretching. For the next 1.5 miles, the player sprints from one tree to the next and then jogs from one tree to the next, mimicking what happens in a game.

A good coach will make sure that their team is in soccer shape. All the skills and tactical advice you give your team will not mean a thing if your players cannot cover the ground in an adequate manner. Do not overlook fitness. A simple exercise like the one below will work.

At intervals in your practice session, have your players line up on the 18-yard line. On your call, they sprint to the halfway line and back in 15 seconds. If one player does not get back in 15 seconds, the rep does not count (use your discretion on this as you may have a player that cannot do it). You can add a cone that is five yards closer (line 1) for your slower players or 5 yards further away (line 3) for your faster players. You can also add lines 1, 2, and 3 to test your players' mental toughness and team mentality. If a player gives it their best effort and can only get to line 1 and back in 15 seconds, then they are no different than a player who can get to line 3 and back in 15 seconds. Over a season,

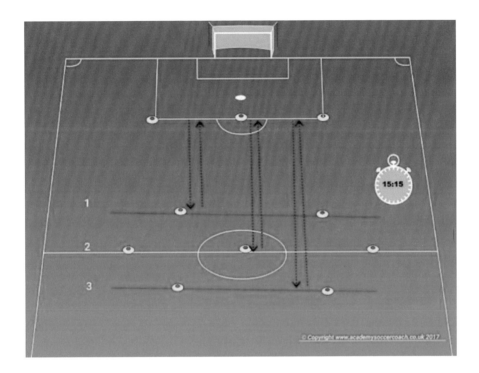

can the player getting to line 1 manage to make it to line 2? After completing the sprint, the players then get 15 seconds to rest before doing another one. Start with five sets and then gradually move to ten. Once a good fitness level is reached, your practice sessions should be sufficient to keep up the fitness levels as long as players are still doing it at home. Speed, agility, and quickness (SAQ) are also encouraged. Give the players ladder work or coordination running techniques. Use these exercises as part of your warm-up.

Ladder exercises

One foot lift, one foot rest

1. Start with your feet at the right side of the ladder.

2. Move up the right side of the ladder by putting your left foot in the ladder and keeping the right foot on the outer side of the ladder.

3. Pump your arms.

4. Your left leg performs a high knee lift in each square while the right leg stays low.

5. Repeat this pattern for the full length of the ladder.

6. When you return, switch sides and work the right leg.

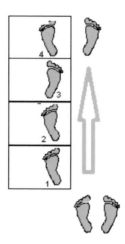

High knee step, one foot in

1. Start with your feet hip-width apart at the bottom of the ladder.

2. Step into the first square with your **left** foot, immediately followed by your **right** foot into the next square.

3. Pump your arms by your side as you perform high knee lifts.

4. Repeat this pattern in a fluid motion for the length of the ladder.

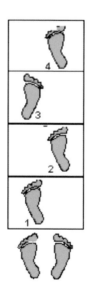

High knee step, two feet in

1. Start with both feet outside.

2. Step into the first square with your **left** foot, immediately followed by your right foot.

3. Using this 1-2 motion, do the same in all the parts of the ladder.

4. Pump your arms by your side and high knee lifts.

5. Repeat this pattern in fluid motion for the length of the ladder with one foot stepping in each part of the ladder

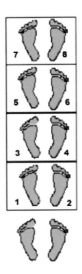

Hopscotch

1. Start with your feet hip-width apart at the bottom of the ladder.

2. Jump up and land in the first square on the left foot.

3. Immediately hop off of the left foot and land with both feet in the second square.

4. Immediately jump off of both feet and land in the next square on your right foot.

5. Immediately hop off of your right foot and land on both feet in the next square.

6. Repeat this pattern for the full length of the ladder.

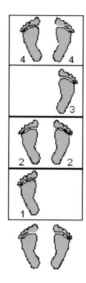

Double hopscotch

1. Start with your feet hip-width apart at the bottom of the ladder.

2. Jump into the first square with both feet.

3. Jump to the next square but put your feet outside the ladder.

4. Repeat this pattern in a fluid motion for the length of the ladder.

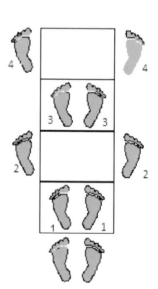

Two in, two out

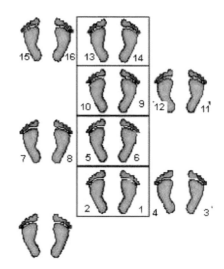

1. Start with both feet outside and to the left of the first square.

2. Step into the first square with your **right** foot first, immediately followed by your left foot in a 1-2 motion.

3. Step out of the square to the **right** with your right foot, followed by your left foot.

4. Now step diagonally into the second square with the left foot leading, always keeping the same 1-2 motion.

5. Step out to the left of the second square with your left foot and repeat for the full length of the ladder.

Hop

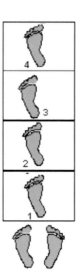

1. Start with your feet hip-width apart at the bottom of the ladder.

2. Hop on your left foot through the full length of the ladder.

3. When you return, hop on the opposite foot.

4. Repeat this pattern for the full length of the ladder.

Five count

1. Start with your feet hip-width apart at the bottom of the ladder.

2. Step out to the right of the first square with your right foot and place your left foot in the first square.

3. Bring your right foot into the first square, then step into the second square with your left foot immediately followed by the right foot.

4. Count these first five steps in a 1-2-3-4-5 manner.

5. Reverse the sequence by stepping out to the left of the third square with your left foot.

6. Repeat for the full length of the ladder.

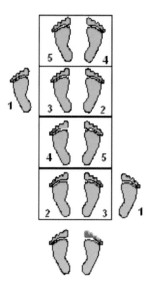

Side step

1. Stand facing the side of the ladder with both feet outside of the first square.

2. Step into the first square with your **right** foot first, immediately followed by your left foot in a 1-2 motion.

3. Step outside the first square with your right foot first, followed by your left in a 1-2 motion.

4. Now step into the second square with the right foot leading, always keeping the same 1-2 motion.

5. Repeat for the full length of the ladder.

6. When you return, face the other way and move through the ladder starting with your left foot.

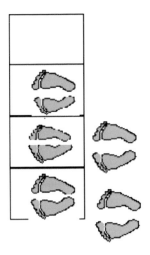

180-degree twist

1. Start with your back to the ladder with your left foot in the first square and your right foot out.

2. Perform a 180-degree twist.

3. Your right foot is now in the first square and your left foot is out.

4. Perform a 180-degree twist to the next square. Now your left foot is in the second square and your right foot is out.

5. Repeat for the full length of the ladder.

6. When you return, start with your right foot in the first square.

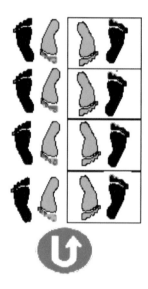

Skier

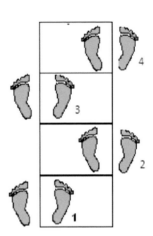

1. Start with your feet hip-width apart at the bottom of the ladder with your right foot in the first square and your left foot out.

2. Hop across to the next square so that your right foot is out and your left foot is in.

3. Repeat for the full length of the ladder.

4. When you return, start with your left foot in the first square.

The fighter

1. Start with your feet hip-width apart with your back to the ladder.

2. Hop in with your left foot and then hop out. Your right foot stays out. Mimic a boxer when they are shadowboxing.

3. Repeat this pattern for the full length of the ladder.

4. When you return, do the exercise using the right foot.

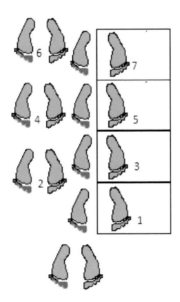

RHYTHM OF A PRACTICE SESSION

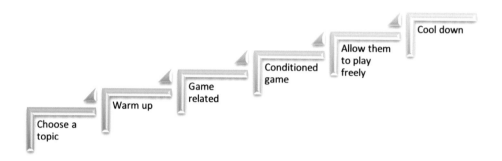

1. Plan your practice session

Make sure the topic or theme is relevant to the ability of your group. It is important to settle on a single topic when putting the practice plan together. This will provide a clear focus for the session, which should translate into a more effective practice on the field for the players. Arrive early and set up the field to eliminate players waiting around between activities while the next on is being set up.

2. Start the practice on time

The warm up can be many different things like ladder work, street soccer, handball, and so on. If there is an element of team jogging and dynamic stretching, get a couple of the players to conduct the warm-up. This will bond the group together and teach leadership. This sets the tone for the practice session ahead. It does not necessarily need to be related to the topic or theme.

3. Get the players focused on the topic

The exercise is performed under some pressure, but not so much pressure that the players struggle to have success. If this activity is too difficult and the players get frustrated and can't find a rhythm, the success of the conditioned game activity will suffer. Be prepared to make the area larger or tone down the level of difficulty. You want success!

4. Relate this to the topic

The coach MUST focus on teaching points related to the theme selected for your session. Practice should include a complex activity that places players in an environment where they are forced to make decisions quickly and to perform techniques under game-like pressures. It has a high resemblance to the game itself in that the players are attacking and defending in a directional manner.

5. Free play

Let the players play with very little coaching. See if they have learned anything from the session.

6. Make time

I know many do not have time for this but it's important. It could range from a full team stretch, a jog across the field or a simple check in with the group to provide closure to the training session.

PHASE I PRACTICE SESSIONS
Dribbling and ball mastery

For this phase of development, keep it fun and simple. You should tell the players what the practice session is about but do not overcomplicate it. The priority at this age is to incorporate ideas on work ethic, behavior, and enjoyment. Have three phases of the practice:

1. A fun warm-up.

2. A game-related practice.

3. A 4v4 game at the end.

A practice that lasts an hour is sufficient for this age group.

Players at this age can still get a sense of the coach's personality. They understand and learn if they see a hard-working coach who has structured practice sessions. Your practice session needs to be engaging and constantly on the go. Below is an example of a structured practice on dribbling.

The coach arrives at the field 20-30 minutes before practice and sets up for the whole practice session, if possible. Start on time. If you said practice began at 6PM, start practice as soon as your watch gets to 6PM. You are planting the seed for encouraging players and parents to be on time.

Start with a fun game. You will have players that show up late so starting with a fun game will allow the latecomers to turn up and join in with the game. There's nothing worse than players arriving late when you are in the middle of your technical session causing you to keep explaining the exercise to them.

Below is a practice focused on ball mastery and dribbling. As you will see, the players get lots of touches on the ball and the exercise is the teacher.

Part 1: Sit-down tag

The size of the area depends on how many players you have (20 x 20 is shown). Designate two players to be taggers and give them with a colored pinnie to wear. The rest of the players have a ball.

1. The players with a ball dribble around the playing area. The taggers run around inside the area and attempt to tag the players.

2. If a player gets tagged, they sit on their soccer ball.

3. To free these players they must be tagged on the shoulder by a dribbling player. The coach can free players, too, if it is easy for the taggers.

4. See if the taggers can get every player to be sitting down.

Coaching points

- Close ball control
- Awareness of players sitting down and the taggers.

Part 2

Players are divided into two teams, and the size of the area is 25 x 30. The coach has all the soccer balls. Each team stands in their goal with their arms linked.

1. Each player is numbered 1-4. (or more as necessary).

2. The coach calls out a number and serves in the ball.

3. The player with that number from each team enters the field, plays a 1v1 and attempts to score on the opposition's goal.

4. The remaining players stay linked together and act as a large goalkeeper. If they break the chain, then a goal is awarded to the other team.

Variation

The coach can call two numbers to create a 2v2.

Coaching points

- 1v1 dribbling skills

- Teamwork and communication (goalkeeper)

Now have them play a 4v4 game; normal soccer rules apply.

1. Teach the players when to dribble, when to pass, and when to shoot.

2. Do not overcoach.

3. Let them figure things out for themselves.

4. Step in if you see an opportunity to coach, but make it quick. Demonstrate, ask the player, and then allow them to execute it.

5. Players will very rarely pass the ball back. If you see that moment, teach it.

PHASE II PRACTICE SESSIONS
Ball control and passing

For this phase of development, the practices are still enjoyable. The word enjoyable often gets overlooked. As long as you are taking part in soccer—whether you are 5 years old or 55 years old—it has to be enjoyable. I stopped playing at the age of 45 because I was not enjoying it any more.

If you participate in anything and you are improving, playing with good people, and having some success, this is enjoyment. This is what coaches mean when they say "We want the players to have fun." It does not mean you are going to run around playing hide and seek or that players will be allowed to goof around, but I can get more out of players who enjoy the sport.

Below are sessions focused on ball control and passing. The sessions are a little more challenging and are related to the game.

Part 1

The size of the area is 20 x 20 for two teams of seven players (4v3). The green team has one ball, while each player on the yellow team has a ball.

1. The yellow team dribble their balls in the playing area and attempt to get in the way of the green team.

2. The green team attempt to pass their ball in the playing area.

3. Players CANNOT touch the other teams ball.

Variation

Switch roles

Coaching points

- The players that are keeping possession quickly find space.

- Note the weight, accuracy, and timing of the pass.

- Note the body shape when receiving the ball. If the player receiving the ball does not see an open player, move the ball with a good first touch.

- Dribbling players should keep up the intensity.

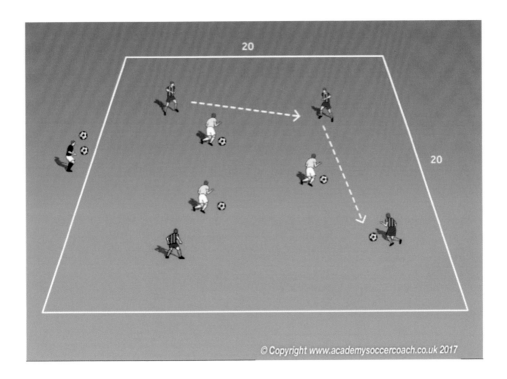

Part 2

The size of the area is 20 x 20 split in two (i.e., 20 x 10). Eight players are shown with two defenders on the outside and three attackers occupying each 20 x 10 area. The coach has all the soccer balls.

1. The coach serves in a ball. A defender enters that playing area. The team in possession can move the ball into the opposite area once they have completed three or more passes.

2. Once they do that, the defender leaves the area. A new defender now enters the opposite area where the ball was played and play continues as before.

3. If the defender wins the ball, then the coach restarts the game.

4. Switch defenders with attackers.

Variation

If you play with more players, you can send in two defenders.

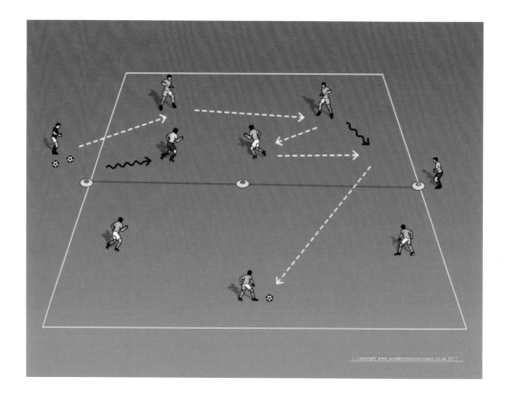

Coaching points

- Angles of support Communication Passing

- First touch Body shape

Part 3

The size of the area is the same as above. Make two teams of 4v4 as shown (you can play with more players). The coach has all the balls. Each team occupies one half of the field.

1. The coach passes the ball to the blue team.

2. Two players (or one player to start with) from the yellow team enter the playing area and attempt to retrieve the ball. If they win possession they must try and pass it to their two team mates in the opposite zone. If they do that, they then quickly move back into their zone.

3. Two blue players now go in and attempt to get the ball back.

4. If the ball goes out of bounds off a defender, the offensive team keeps possession of the ball.

Coaching points

- Angles of support Communication Passing
- First touch

Teaching 7v7 in a practice environment

When it's game day be patient with the team's sense of positioning and the roles they play on the field. This is new to them. How can young players understand a system if you are not teaching it at your practice sessions?

Here is how you conduct a functional practice on the system you are playing. It should be no longer than 10-15 minutes. Do it before the group has a game at the end of practice. It gives the players a general idea of what is needed to play the system.

The system of play for 7v7 is 1-2-3-1.

1. Set up two different colored cones on a regular sized 7v7 field (45 x60).
2. The red cones are for when the team is defending and the yellow cones are for when the team is attacking.
3. Place the players on the defending cones. If you have more than seven players, more than one player can occupy a cone. (Players should link arms if there are more than one on a cone.)
4. Call out "Attack!" and the players move to the attacking yellow cones. For example, the goalkeeper will move to the edge on the penalty area, the two center backs will move higher up the field, and so on.
5. Call out "Defend!" and the players retreat by quickly jogging backwards to their defensive positions.

Coaching points

- Keep it quick and simple.
- Explain to the players that this exercise will give them a general idea of what playing 7v7 looks like.

After about 10-15 minutes of this exercise, let the players play a game. Look for signs that they understand field awareness.

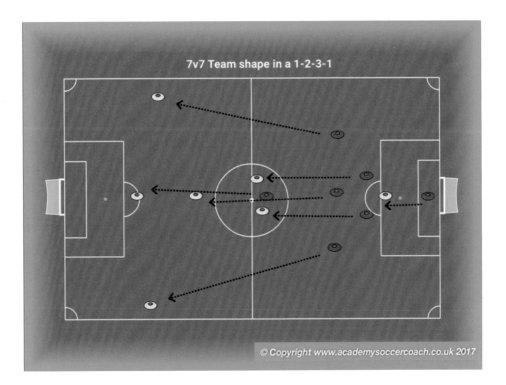

7v7 Team shape in a 1-2-3-1

© Copyright www.academysoccercoach.co.uk 2017

PHASE III PRACTICE SESSIONS
Switching play and overlaps

You are still incorporating technical work in your practice session. The tactical demands on the players are growing.

Following is a session focused on switching play and overlaps, which shows your players the value of switching the point of attack.

Part 1

The size of the area is 30 x 20. Player A starts the exercise.

1. Player A passes to player B and starts to overlap player B. Player B passes the ball wide to player C who passes the ball to player A.

2. Player A overlaps, receives the ball, and passes to player D. Players A, B, and C join any cone at the opposite end.

3. Player D starts the exercise coming the opposite way and so on.

Coaching points

- Timing and weight of pass

- Movement and communication

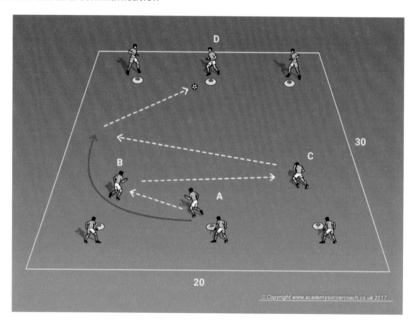

Encourage the players to try all the different aspects of the exercise. When the players complete the sequence and return to the opposite end, they switch positions and stand at a different cone.

Variation 1

Player A runs the opposite direction to their pass. Player A passes to B, B passes to C, and C passes to A who is overlapping player C. Player A then passes to player D.

Variation 2

Player A passes wide to either player B or player C. They then pass the ball back to player A who starts moving forward with the ball. Players B and C overlap central player A. Player A decides who to pass the ball to.

With the number of variations to this exercise, you may want to move to a conditioned game after the players have finished this technical exercise.

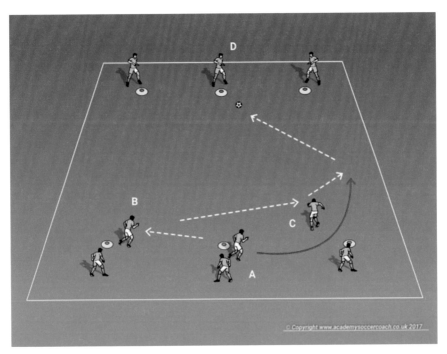

Variation 1

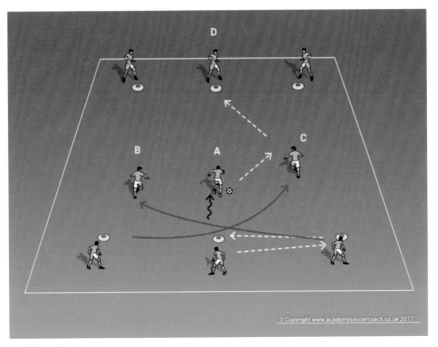

Variation 2

Part 2

The size of the area is half a field. Place three small goals at the end lines for teams to attack. Each team has one player staying behind the three goals at the end line.

1. Normal rules apply.

2. To score, the ball has to be passed through one of the three goals.

3. The sweeper behind the goal moves along the end line to stop a goal being scored. This encourages the players to move the ball quickly and switch the point of attack.

Coaching points

- Quick ball movement

- Movement off the ball and communication Quality passing to feet or into space

© Copyright www.academysoccercoach.co.uk 2017

Part 3

Allow the players to play a game. Stand back and watch to see if they have learned anything from the first two parts of the practice. Step in to coach when needed. Also, look for the moments when the players carry out an overlap or switch play. Step in to praise that moment. Do not continue to coach the negative. Coach and praise positive play too.

PHASE IV PRACTICE SESSIONS

Compact defending

You are still incorporating technical work in your practice session. The players are now starting to be challenged more tactically and physically.

Following is a session focused on balanced defending. Emphasize to the players that defending is a skill. No matter how good you are at attacking, you still need to be just as good at defending. This is a great session which shows your players the value of defending as a unit.

Part 1

The size of the area is 24 x 25 (i.e., two 12 x 25 areas). Set up a 4v4 with two or three target players outside the area. The coach has all the soccer balls.

1. The four players cannot come outside their playing area.

2. The coach serves in a ball. The yellow team passes the ball to each other looking for an opportunity to pass to the target players.

3. The object of the exercise is that the back four players (blue team) move as a unit and block the passes to the target player. Each blue player moves forward to press the player opposite without going in the opposite area.

4. If a pass is blocked or a pass is made to the target players the game continues with the target player passing the ball in to the opposition.

5. Change target players.

Coaching points

- Team-work and communication
- Positional sense, angles, and balance of the four players

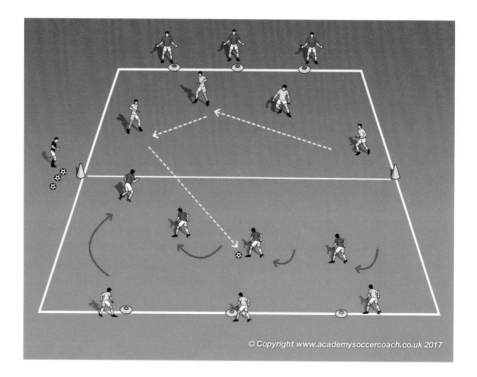

© Copyright www.academysoccercoach.co.uk 2017

Variation

Play 3v1 in the playing areas. The team in possession of the ball are pressured by one defender while the other three defenders move as a unit to block the through balls.

The size of the area is 36 x 40 with two 15-yard end zones and a 10-yard center zone. Use 15-18 players split into three teams. Two teams are in the end zone and a defending team is in the middle zone. The figure below shows 15 players organized in a 5v5v5.

1. The coach plays the ball to the yellow team.

2. Two defending blue players enter the area. The yellow team keeps possession and attempts to pass the ball to the red team. The ball can be transferred after three or more passes from the yellow team.

3. The defending blue team makes play predictable. The two players inside the end zone press the ball while the other three cover and balance and block passing lanes.

4. The ball cannot go above head height.

5. If the defending team wins the ball, you can either switch them with the team that lost possession of the ball or just reset and start the exercise again.

Variation

Switch defenders.

Coaching points

- Defense
- Communication
- Being compact
- Predictable play
- Moving as a unit
- Arcing runs

Part 2

The size of the area is half a field or a full field, depending on the number of players. Have two small target goals at each end as shown. Teams score by passing through these small target goals. You can work one team on defense and one on offense, or you can play it as a game and coach both teams on compact defending.

1. Look for the defending team to slide and make the area where the ball is compact.

2. See if the players can use the coaching points from the previous two exercises.

Coaching points

- Communication

- Working as a unit

- Reactions

As you can see here, the blue team is not defending these two players tight. They are making the area compact.

Tactical defending practice

Defend the penalty box

Set up the playing area as shown in the figure. Six 6 x 3 boxes are marked down the side of the 6-yard area extending to the edge of the penalty box. The server is inside a 6 x 4 box marked 22 yards from the goal. One yellow player occupies each box, and a 2v2 is played inside the penalty area with a goalkeeper in the goal. The two red players are defending the goal. Yellow players on the outside are one touch only and the offside rule is in play.

The objective of the exercise is for the yellow players to keep the ball and create shooting opportunities. The red defenders track the play and defend quickly to block passes or shots. Red defenders score by blocking a shot and score two points if they win possession and pass it to the server.

The server passes the ball to alternate sides. The yellow outer players can pass to each other (see figure 2).

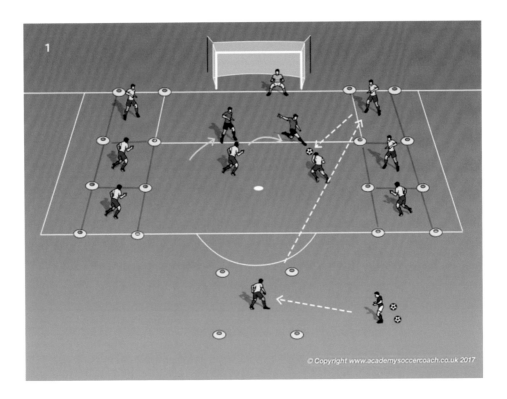

© Copyright www.academysoccercoach.co.uk 2017

Coaching points

- Look at angles and distance other.

- They must try to see the player and ball at all times and keep an open body stance.

The outer players combine passes. This challenges the two defenders defending the penalty box.

Now increase the size of the playing area and play 5v5 in the central area (see figure 3). This challenges the defenders more because the yellow attackers have more space to run in behind. The defenders and the goalkeeper need to be aware of the space behind the defense. Encourage the outer players to cross the ball. This will create realistic scenarios that happen in games.

It is important to play a game at the end of the practice. Figure 4 shows the group playing 7v7 with the red players defending the large goal. When the red players win the ball, they attempt to score in either of the small goals.

Reverse the role of the teams. Yellow team now gets an opportunity to defend the large goal.

The practice creates realistic challenges that can happen in and around the penalty area. The session is intense, so hopefully when it comes to the pressures of the real game, your players will be ready and confident to compete and make smart decisions.

The ball is played wide and then crossed into the danger area.

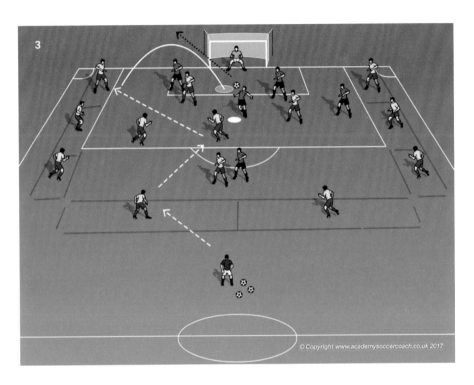

Coaching points

- Allow your group to play at the end of the practice.

- Look for signs of the players understanding of the topic.

Tactical midfield practice

Movement and forward runs

Start with 5v5 in a 40 x 40 area. Have the forwards position themselves as target players on the outside (as shown in figure 1). These target plays have a one- or two-touch passing restriction.

The team in possession (red) must complete four passes within their team before they can pass to any target player. If they manage to do this, they score a point. If the yellow team wins the ball, they attempt to do the same.

Coaching points

- Create quick angles of play around the ball.

- If your position is cut off by the opposition, quickly move and support in another area. This will involve players rotating their positions with teammates.

Once the ball has been played to a target player, the possession team quickly moves to support the target player (see figure 2). The target player has a two-touch restriction, so support has to be quick and players have to show a good angle of support.

If the target player passes the ball back to the red team, then they attempt to make another four passes (or more) before they pass to a target player again.

If you want to rotate the target players, you can. After four or more passes, the red team passes to a target player.

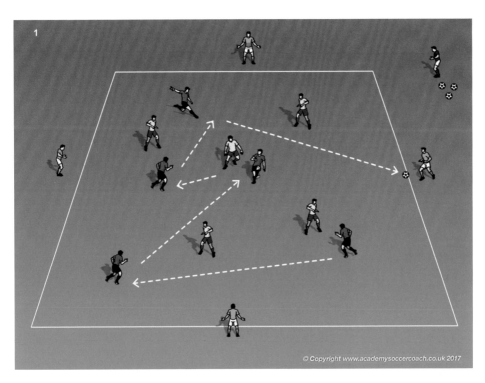

Coaching points

- Movement

- Forward runs

Now use a full field but section it off. Mark it level with the outside 18-yard box and have a 10-yard zone occupied by one of the target players (as shown in figure 3). Goalkeepers are placing in the goals.

5v5 is played in the central zone. Each team is assigned a goal to attack.

The conditions remain the same with four passes or more before passing to the target player.

Once the ball is passed to a target player, one of the attacking players breaks out of the central zone and supports him. The target player can either turn and shoot or pass the ball to the running midfield player. If the yellow team scores, they receive the ball from the coach. If they miss, the coach passes the ball to the red team.

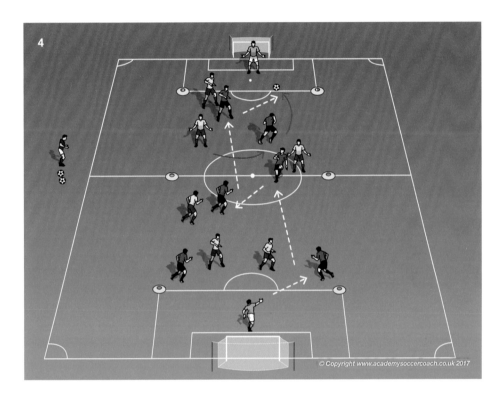

Remove the target players and add one to each of the teams. Remove the 10-yard target zone and allow the players to play (see figure 4). If you have more players you can play full field and your system of play (4-4-2, 4-3-3, etc.).

Coaching points

Look to see if the players recognize when and where and who. When does the team pass to the target man? Where do they support from? Who has moved into the best position to receive the ball?

Tactical wing practice

Creativity from your wide players

Set up on half a field as shown in figure 1. Set up eight mannequins that represent a back four (you can also use cones). With this practice, use the fullbacks, wide players, strikers, and goalkeepers; you can also run it as a team practice if you want. This is a technical exercise that shows the wide players various combinations of play.

Combination A

The ball is played out wide, and the receiving wide player cuts inside to beat the fullback, playing a disguised pass to the striker. The striker times his run to stay onside and take a shot at goal.

Combination B

The ball is played to the wide player who cuts inside and plays a give and go with the forward before taking a shot at goal. Have the players move to the next cone after the activity is over. (See figure 2.)

Combination C

The ball is played to the wide player. The wide player cuts inside and plays the ball to the moving striker. The player who passed to the wide player continues his run. The forward plays the ball wide to the third-man running. The wide player is now attacking the front post and supported by the striker. The fullback crosses the ball.

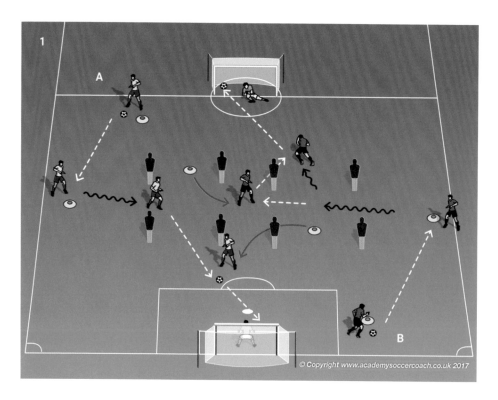

Combination D

The ball is played wide, and the wing plays a wide give and go and crosses the ball for the forward. The inverted wings create confusion for the opposition.

Coaching points

- Creativity from your wide players.
- Use other combinations that suite your style of play.

After completing several different combinations, move to a game-related exercise. Play on half a field marked with cones that just wider than the penalty area. The field is marked into two halves. There are two mannequins (cones) placed on either side of the halfway line (see figure 3).

8v8 is played with 3v2 in favor of defenders in each half plus two wide players from each team on the outside. The 3v2 players stay in their own half. The yellow defenders have the ball. They are supported on the outside by the wide players. Once the ball is played wide, both wide players become active and move through the mannequins or cones to create a 4v3 in the attacking half. If the red players win the ball, they can start the counterattack. The wide players only become active when they or their opposite wide player receives the ball.

Then finish by playing on half a field with three target gates on the halfway line and a goal with a goalkeeper at the opposite end. One team attack the big goals and one attacks the three small goals. The team attacking the gates must score by dribbling the ball through any of the three gates. The coach now has an opportunity to coach their style of play.

Coaching points

- Look for signs of learning from your players.
- Watch how creative your wide players will be. Do they understand their movement?

The opposite wide player joins in with the attack.

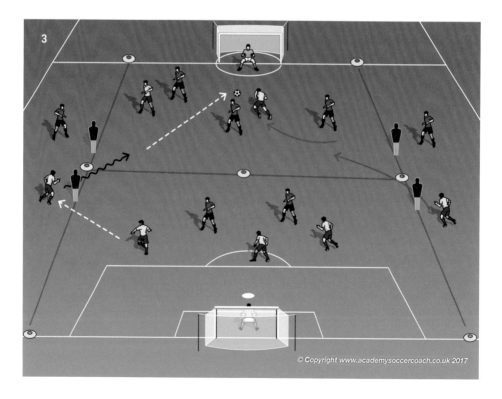

Tactical attacking practice

Reacting in the box

Set up as shown in figure 1 with 12 players grouped into four teams of three players. Only one ball is used. Six players are on the outside, and a 3v3 is played in the middle. The 3v3 players play man-on-man and can only compete against the player they are assigned to. The team in possession can pass the ball between them or they can use an outside player. If a player passes to an outside player, that player and his opponent have to sprint around the outside player that received the ball and then rejoin the game. Rotate the inside players with the players on the outside. This is a good warm-up because it is geared toward getting the players mentally ready for an intense practice session.

Then progress the session into the penalty area. There are three goals, and each goal is assigned to a team. (You can use three large goals with goalkeepers, if available.) Here we show one large goal with a goalkeeper and two smaller goals without a goalkeeper.

Play 4v4v4. Teams are looking to score on the other two goals while defending their own. Run for three periods of 5 minutes and rotate each team after 5 minutes so they get to defend all three goals. Add the score at the end.

Coaching points

- Look for field awareness and reactions in the box.

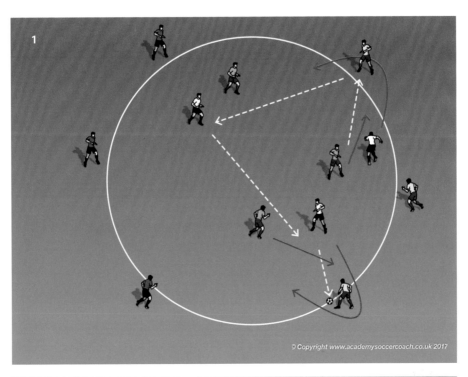

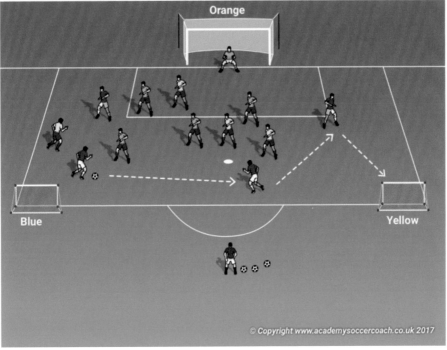

Reacting in the box

Advance the session by playing 6v6 in a 24 x 20 area. The playing area is split in half. Set up two large goals with goalkeepers. In each half, there are four players, one goalkeeper, and one opposition player (as shown in figure 3). The coach has all the soccer balls. The coach serves the ball to the yellow team. The yellow team stays in the 12 x 20 area and keeps possession. When they get an opportunity to shoot, they take a shot from inside their half. The yellow player inside the opposite half looks for rebounds. The single player attempts to win the ball back, and if they do win the ball, they can either shoot or play the ball back to their team. Rotate the single player. The single player can also be used as a wall pass player.

Then move to a small-sided game inside two 18-yard areas and have one team attacking a large goal and the other team attacking three small goals. When scoring on the three small goals, it must be a one-touch finish. Allow the team to play and watch to see if you are seeing signs of learning.

Switch roles and allow the blue team to attack the large goal. If you have time, you can move the practice to a "normal" game of soccer. Players enjoy the time to play at the end of practice.

© Copyright www.academysoccercoach.co.uk 2017

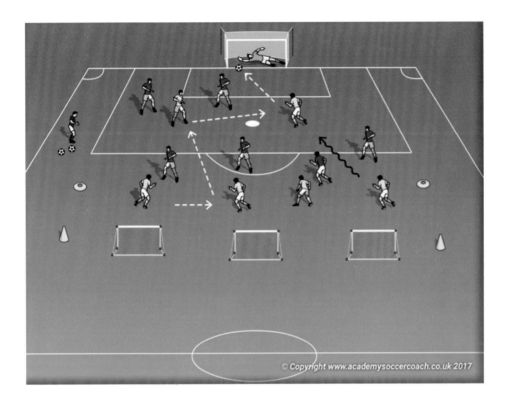

The yellow player shoots while the yellow player in the opposite box looks for rebounds.

Coaching points

- Allow the teams to play and watching to see if there are any signs of learning.

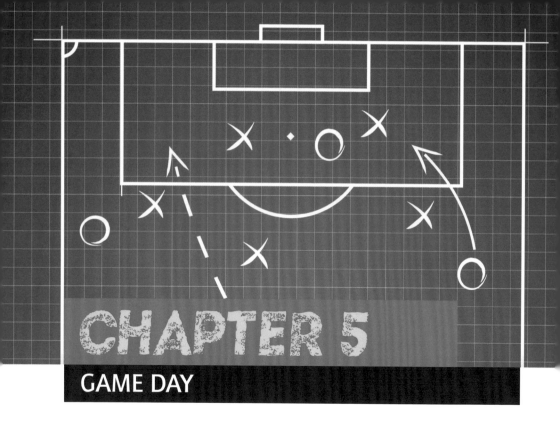

CHAPTER 5
GAME DAY

COACH PERFORMANCE, NOT RESULTS

The process

The majority of clubs just let their coaching staff play whatever system they want. There is no one monitoring the coach and the team. There is no structure for a long-term vision or goal. The vision is usually just *win the game!* In a development philosophy, the teams (boys and girls) play the same system right through to U12. When the games are 4v4, 7v7, and 9v9, all the coaching staff play the same system. The coaches are allowed to change it up every now and then to allow the players to figure it out, but they always revert to the blueprint. Every player must understand the system for each age group. Don't forget that these are young players and they need to walk before they can run. Getting them settled into a structure will enhance their development because:

1. Players feel comfortable in a structured setting.

2. If a coach needs to stand in to coach one of the other teams, they are speaking the same language to the players.

3. If a player gets moved to another team (for whatever reason), they can fit straight into the system.

4. Players can comfortably rotate into other positions because they have learned from their teammates and heard the coach using the same instructions when discussing other positions.*

5. Players gain more confidence and an understanding of the game.

6. The transition to other systems once the team grows to 9v9 and 11v11 will be a lot easier.

7. It is a lot harder for the opposition if your players are organized and understand their roles.

Game day is the best day of the week for your players. You want to excel at your practice sessions and have the discipline to use game day as an extra teaching and learning opportunity. Your style of play is designed to be successful against the opposition. It is designed so that your players understand their roles on the field. The concept of your system is not based on positions or formations; instead it enables players to understand the game while being successful in terms of results. While we develop the players, we want them to feel a sense of achievement. If young players are not seeing a reward for their efforts, you will not be able to keep the group together.

This development blueprint system is not designed to give you more time on the ball to move it around the pitch; it is designed to make it more difficult for the opponent and easier for your players to understand. You want your players to be brave and this means taking the initiative, controlling the game, and imposing your style on your opponents with the objective of winning for the sake of the team and not for the sake of the coach or the parents.

It is a rule when developing a team culture that players must arrive to the game on time. Warm-ups start 30 minutes before kickoff. Players that **do not** make the warm-up on time do not start. Monitor the warm-up. You have to show the team that you have expectations.

While the coach names the starting lineup, the players form a mini version of the tactical formation that the coach has chosen. Below the coach has chosen a 1-2-1-3-2 (9v9) and he or she gives the players coaching points for each position. This enables all the players to understand how the formation looks and what roles they have in the game.

---

*This blueprint philosophy does not believe every player should try every position. This is left to the coach's discretion. You have to build up the players' confidence first before moving them to unfamiliar positions. You will get players that can play all positions, but you will also get players that are best suited to playing in one position for now. You have to make sure that your long-term goal is to get them to play a couple of positions. The key is finding the right time to allow this to happen. Rushing the process can ruin it for young players.

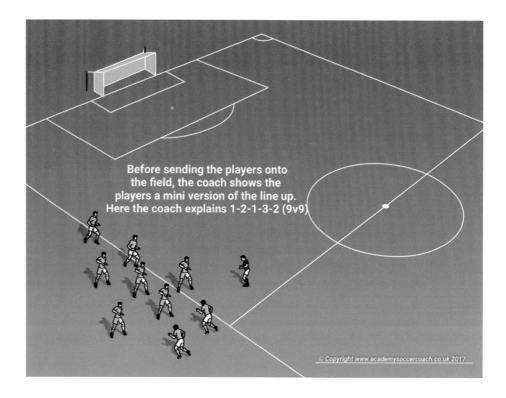

Before sending the players onto the field, the coach shows the players a mini version of the line up. Here the coach explains 1-2-1-3-2 (9v9)

© Copyright www.academysoccercoach.co.uk 2017

Once the team goes out onto the field, it is in their hands. Allow them to play and work on their soccer IQ. You have worked hard all week on the practice field. You have coached the team on how you want them to perform. Now let them go onto the field and figure out the game. Take notes during every game. If you take too many notes (which can happen at the youth level) and you do not have enough time at the half to cover everything, try and cover the top three most important ones. Ask your players what they see.

The following are things you can concentrate on during the game:

- Spot the dangers or opportunities before they happen. The only instructions from the sidelines should involve moving players or telling them to get goal side or to move forward.

- What formation are the opposition playing?

- Is the opposition coach aware of your system?

- Do the players know where their teammates are going to be when they receive the ball? Thinking ahead and making decisions before they get the ball are very important.

- Will the formation that you are using exploit the opposition's tactics?

- Do the players look like they understand the system?

- Playing formations does not guarantee a result. Players have to be willing to put in the effort. The anticipation when winning or losing the ball are key factors in the game. What reaction do the players have to these two scenarios?

- When the team attacks, the defenders stay focused. When possession is won, the coach will look to see if the defenders are focused. Are the fullbacks offering support? Is the opponent out of balance?

- When the team defends, the forwards stay focused. When possession is lost the coach will look to see if the forwards are focused and if the wide players are getting goal side.

- Does the opposition have a star player who is affecting the game?

- Players must have an impact on the game. If they are not passing the ball well or they are struggling with the technical side of the game, then they must make sure that their opponent has no impact on the game.

- Be first to the loose ball on all set pieces and clearances for and against.

- Keep an eye out for good communication from all. Young players will generally just focus on their own task. They also have to learn to see what their teammates are doing. Are any of their teammates struggling? Does a teammate need encouragement?

- If a player moves out of position to impact the game, who will offer cover for that player?

- Players know there are two kinds of passes: to *feet* or to *space*. A player that calls for the ball may not be the right decision when passing the ball. The player on the ball has to recognize the potential dangers.

- At U12 and below, you will need to move your players around the field both offensively and defensively with verbal instructions. What you should not be doing is telling players when to pass or shoot.

- The use of your substitutes is important. *Do not* stack your bench with the weaker players. You have to give all your players sufficient playing time. If you start the game with your best team, then the dynamics of the team will change dramatically when substitutions are made. This will be the coach's decision as each opponent and game will be different. **At all levels of youth soccer, players should get at least 25 minutes of playing time** (if the player's attitude is good).

- When possession is lost, the team takes a good defensive position and attempts to win the ball back quickly. If opportunities to win the ball back quickly are denied, players should recover quickly to organize a compact defensive block behind the ball (including the goalkeeper).

- Make sure the information given to the players at halftime and after the game is productive. Explain to them in a way they can understand. If you have not worked on the things that you are telling them, how will they know how to execute?

It's not just about the result.

Game day post-match thoughts:

- Keep everything in perspective.

- If the team played well and won, celebrate.

- If the team played well and lost, this is disappointing, but there are lots of positives to focus on.

- If the team played poorly and own, they still need to improve despite the good result.

- If the team played poorly and lost, with hard work at practice, they will get it right. Teamwork!

Game day: 4v4

The perfect squad number is six players per team. If possible, try to avoid taking more than this number. The players need quality playing time.

Play a 1-3 formation (see figure 1). Even at this age, players need structure and guidelines to follow. Start warming up 20 minutes before kickoff. Choose the team from the players who attend practices and who also turn up to the game on time. It is an injustice to the players who are on time if you start the players who are late.

Keep game day instructions simple. Each group of players and each individual will follow the instructions at a different pace. You have to understand the level of the player you are coaching. Do not treat them like adults. The coach has to teach the players in a way they can understand. Do not overcomplicate the coaching. When playing 4v4, the team will line up in a 1-3 formation. The defender will be rotated and will not always play at the back. In this system, all the players can play in every one of the four positions on the field.

The defender will be encouraged to stay back and push up to the half when the team is on the attack. Encourage this player to run with the ball out from the back if the

Figure 1

opportunity arises. One of the other players on the field will be encouraged to offer cover for that defender if they decide to move out from the back with the ball. The three attacking players will be encouraged to find space when you have the ball.

When possession is lost, you teach the players to stand goal side of the opposition and to guard an opposition player when you do not have the ball.

Sideline instructions from the coach should encourage and help the players to get into a position on the field that will help them and the team.

When possession is lost, encourage the players to guard the opposing team. The figure below shows the team quickly returning to defensive shape when the ball is lost. This early stage of teaching defending is critical. You are planting the seed for the future. Do not allow any of the players to get away with this aspect of the game. A little encouragement from the coach to get goal side is totally appropriate; screaming and yelling these instructions is not. That's why you should encourage the players to do it. It starts to teach leadership and the players are hearing it from their teammates, not just the coach (see figure 2).

Figure 2

The same applies when the team has the ball. Get the players to call out "Find space!" The players are encouraged to move away from the opponent and call for the ball. Once again, you are teaching leadership. The work ethic from the players at 4v4 is exactly the same when defending as when attacking. The main focus at this age is not the outcome of the game but on getting the players to understand work ethic, behavior, and teamwork (see figure 3).

Figure 3

Game day: 7v7

The perfect squad number is 10-11 players. If possible, try to avoid taking more than this number. The players need quality playing time. The formation used for 7v7 is 1-2-3-1. The player with the ball has at least three players available for a pass. One behind, one to the side and one ahead of the ball. As the players mature we expect the player on the ball to have more than three supporting players. The 1-2-3-1 formation creates triangles all over the field and enables the players to make lots of diagonal passes (see figure).

The game day instructions for the players are kept simple. Start warming up 30 minutes before kickoff. The team will be chosen from the players who arrive on time for the start of the warm ups. When playing 7v7 the team will line up in a 1-2-3-1 formation.

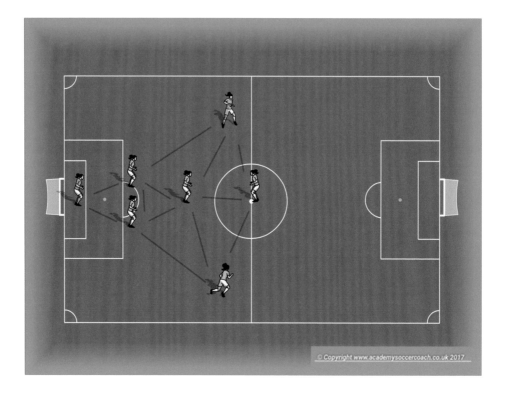

Instructions to the two defenders:

- If the opposition does not have a forward when we are attacking, one of the defenders will step into the middle of the midfield and play as a holding midfield player.

- If they have one forward when we are attacking, one defender will stand in front of the forward and one defender will stand behind the forward. If the opposition clears the ball, then the defender standing in front will hopefully win the ball back to start another attack.

- If they have two forwards both defenders will stand goal side of those forwards.

- When the ball is lost the players need to understand when to mark tight and when to mark lose. If there is one forward, one defender is tight and the other defender is the sweeper.

Instructions to the wide midfielders:

- When possession is lost the wide player gets goal side on the opposition wide player that is closest to their goal if the opposition are playing a 1-3-3 formation.
- At their first opportunity they must run at the defender and try to beat them in a 1 v 1. This will give them an idea of the oppositions defending skills. Are they slow or fast? Can they defend a 1v1?
- Make runs behind the defender. Are they aware of field position?
- Play give and gos with teammates.
- Make quality crosses.

Instructions to the center midfield player:

- Move up and down the field supporting the team when defending and attacking.
- Find pockets of space when your team is in possession.
- Get goal side (behind the ball) when possession is lost.

Instructions to the center forward:

- Stay up front and move sideways to support the play.

A lot of young players at the 7v7 stage usually run back and defend when possession is lost. A lot of teams play 1-3-3 and when you have possession it allows you to move one of your central defenders into a midfield role. This is priceless soccer education for the future of your players. As you can see from the picture below, the dark team has the ball and the defending white team have all retreated on defense. You do not want to leave two or three defenders standing back on defense if the opposition do not have any forwards. If this scenario is in front of you, allow one of the defenders to move into a midfield position while the other stays back and covers the defense. The central midfield player can now be free to support the attack. The opposite wide player comes in and makes diagonal runs into space.

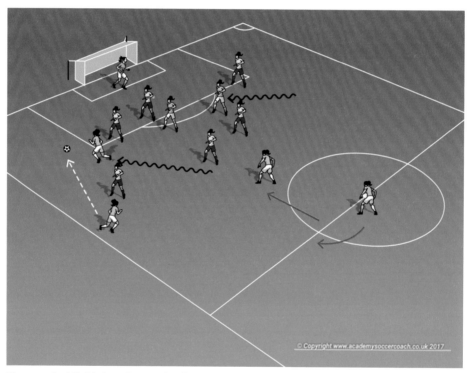

The central midfield player has made a forward run. One of the central defenders steps in as a holding midfield player while the other stays back and moves in relation to the ball.

When defending your team becomes compact (see below) The forward does not retreat and defend with their team mates. The forward stays high and moves side to side in relation to where the ball is.

When possession is lost, the forward stays high. Lateral movement from the lone striker is in relation to the ball.

There is no creativity in the 1-3-3 system. The only problem you may encounter is when the goalkeeper has the ball in their hands. If you leave your forward to deal with the opposition back three then you give the opposition goal-keeper an excellent opportunity to play it out from the back. Many countries have now added a "retreat line" (which is a great rule) when a goal keeper has a goal kick. Below shows you how your players react when the goal-keeper has the ball in their hands.

The central midfield player steps in to help the forward split the back three. The wide players guard the opposition wide player that is closest to their goal.

If you have your players mark 'man for man' then this is a big risk. Yes, this will work if your players are superior to the opposition but you are not teaching team work and cover and balance. Teaching cover and balance (soccer intelligence) will plant the seed for the future.

© Copyright www.academysoccercoach.co.uk 2017

This example shows you what happens when both teams play 1-3-3. Once a 1v1 has been successful, then the defending team is in trouble.

Game day: 9v9

The perfect squad number is 12 or 13 players. If possible, try to avoid taking more than this number. The players need quality playing time. The mentality of players will start to change when you move to 9v9. The results for the games are now posted on websites and the players can look at the tables to see how they compare to the other teams. Players look at the teams who are winning and losing and then figure out which will be easier games. You have to teach the players to ignore the standings and play to their maximum potential. Players have to give it their best effort on that particular day and whatever the result, the players can walk off the field and say they did their best. U11 and U12 football is 9v9 with goalkeepers. The formation used for 9v9 is 1-2-1-3-2.

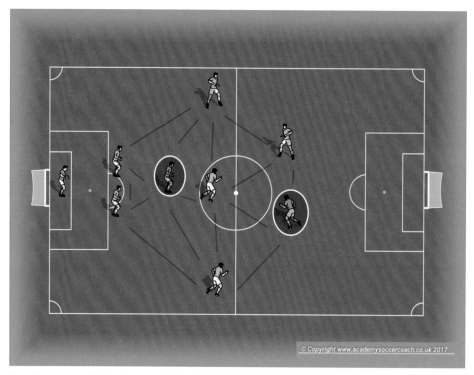

© Copyright www.academysoccercoach.co.uk 2017

Two players are added in these positions when you move to 9v9.

The game day instructions start to become more tactical. Warm-up time is the same as U9 and U10. When playing 9v9, the team will line up in a 1-2-1-3-2 formation. The instructions for the two defenders will be the same as the instructions in 7v7. The opposition is more likely to have at least one forward—and possibly two—whereas at 7v7, this was not the case. The two defenders need to have tactical awareness of when to mark tight and when to mark loose. The coach has to be aware of what the opposition is doing and coach accordingly.

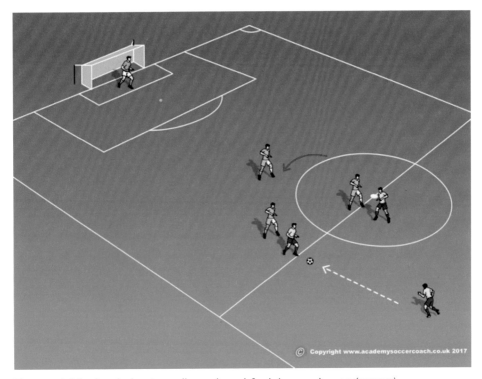

The central defender who is not guarding a player defends loose and covers (sweeper).

Below is a list of coaching points to explain to the players:

- Players must react quickly when possession is won or lost. Win the ball, find space. Lose the ball, get goal side.

- The player with the ball has at least three players supporting their play. One player supports behind, one supports from the side, and one supports forward. This will gradually move to more supporting players as the players mature.

- Play with a holding midfield player.

- Encourage the goalkeeper to play out from the back. If the ball is caught by the goalkeeper, then the two center backs split quickly to the corner of the penalty area because the opposition may be out of balance. One of the midfield players sits in the space created by the two center backs and plays deeper as they may also collect the ball from the goalkeeper. If the goalkeeper does not deliver the ball to any of these three players, then they will quickly return to a more central defensive and midfield position.

- The two defenders must stay focused when you win possession. The two forwards must stay focused when you lose possession. When possession is lost, the forwards defend from the front. Once the ball is in your own attacking third, the forwards look to take up a position on the field so that when the ball is won, the team can get the ball to them.

- If a defender goes on the attack, the best player that is positioned to cover for the attacking defender will do so if needed.

If the opposition play with two strikers, then the teaching moment for the player is when to mark tight and when to mark loose. The following figure demonstrates teaching a flat back two for young players. Teaching this style sets them up for success when moving to 11v11.

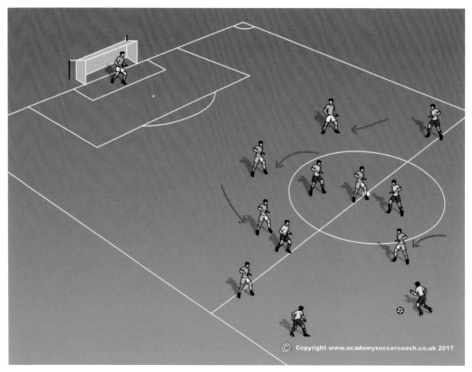

The second central defender defends a little loose. The central defender that is on the same side as the ball is the one who defends tight. The left-sided player also comes inside a little and defends loose.

Encourage your defenders to move out of defense with the ball. The teaching moment is now for a teammate to cover. The following figure shows one of the central midfield players dropping to center back because the defender has moved out of defense with the ball. It may be rare for a center back to make a forward run without the ball— there will be other players on the field who are better suited to that sort of attacking option—but if this does happen, the principles are the same: the central midfield player drops back.

The central midfielder rotates and covers for the center back who has dribbled the ball out from the back.

The above example is a great teaching moment involving soccer intelligence. This whole development philosophy is built around decision making and the above example will give you great satisfaction when you see this happen with your players. It shows an understanding of the game but also shows teamwork. It is even more satisfying when you see young players do this.

The role of the two central midfield players will depend on their style of play and whether you, as a coach, trust them. You should show the players that you trust them. The list below outlines how you want the two central midfield players to play:

- Designate one to play holding midfielder and the other to attack.

- Have them play each position for 15-minute intervals.

- Test their soccer intelligence and allow them to play it as they see it. If one goes, then the other holds.

It is important to remember that games are also learning environments for players. If you are asking a player to do any of the above and you have not worked on it on the practice field, then do not be too quick to criticize. If you try the above and things go wrong, take some responsibility and let the players know that things are fine and you will work more on their positions on the practice field. Creating decision makers will lead to players and coaches getting things wrong. That is how we all learn.

When you are playing in this system, your wide players could possibly get overloaded by the opposing team (e.g., if you are playing against a 1-3-3-2 or a 1-4-3-1). If this is the case, your players need to have the soccer intelligence to deal with it.

Below are directions on how you can deal with your wide player being overloaded.

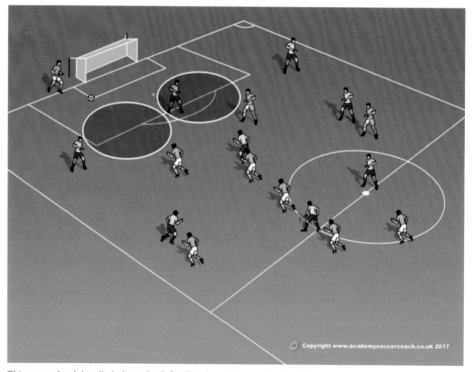

This center back is a little loose in defending in relation to the ball. The two forwards split the three defenders to make it difficult for the opposition to play out from the back.

The image below shows the opposing right defender moving forward. One of your two forwards (strikers) should shift across to defend that player. Your wide midfielder needs to focus on the wide attacking player that is closer to the goal.

If this wide midfield player is not helped by the striker, they will be in 2v1 overload, and they will get exploited by the opposition.

If the forwards have not been alert, then the two central midfielders need to react to help the wide midfielder. Your midfield two should constantly be talking to the two forwards. The forwards have to defend from the front. If they do not put the work in when you lose the ball, the system will break down.

One of the central midfield players has moved across to help the wide midfielder.

This topic of systems can be a very opinionated. When we are developing players, we need to be clear on what system of play works while we are developing the team for the future. Some coaches have short-term goals and play the system that wins them games. The good coaches teach both. They teach a system of play that gets their team results, but that also sets them up for when they move to 9v9 and 11v11.

The systems in this blueprint have worked for me over the last 15 years. I looked at the system from a development point of view: How can you easily explain the system in a way young athletes can understand? I found that the explanations in a development philosophy were easy to comprehend and also very effective.

Game day: 11v11

After forming your players with a development system, you are now ready for 11v11. You are now free to use whatever system suits your group of players. If your players have come through a development system, they will be capable of adapting to the team's system of play. In this section, we are going to show you two systems of play.

1-4-1-3-2 formation

The perfect squad number for 11v11 is 15– or 16 players. If possible, try to avoid taking more than this number. The players need quality playing time. The players that have come through your club's development phases will be capable of adapting to many formations; 3-4-3, 4-3-3, 4-2-3-1, and 4- 1-3-2 will be taught at 11v11. If the team plays 4-1-3-2 then the coach decides if they want one or two holding midfield players. The fullbacks are encouraged to move forward when attacking on their side of the field. If the team is not getting any luck with this system, then switch to 4-3-3. Your players should be ready to switch formations on the fly and each player should understand their role in each formation. Changing formations is also a good way for players to start fresh.

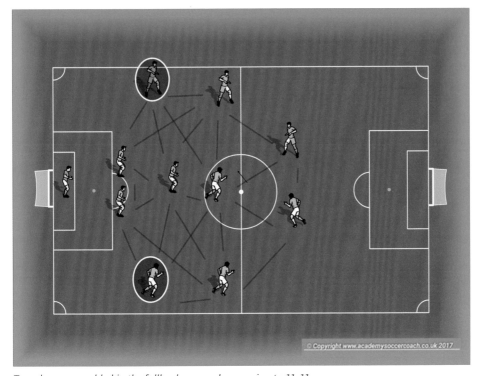

© Copyright www.academysoccercoach.co.uk 2017

Two players are added in the fullback areas when moving to 11v11.

For example, if the team is not getting any success in the first half, then the coach can switch the formation. This change helps young players to approach the second half with a positive attitude. It also helps if the coach can put some of the blame on their own shoulders by telling the players that it was a mistake to play the formation and that they think another formation or strategy would work better. The coach may also need to change the system because of the opposition. Players and coaches need to adapt.

All the game day preparations are the same as what you did at 7v7 and 9v9. Your warm-ups have had some variations over the years, and you will develop the warm-up to the level and needs of your team.

One of the things I enjoyed was watching my fullbacks get forward. As you can see from the system above, we just added two fullbacks from the 9v9 system we played. These two players had been playing wide midfield at 7v7 and 9v9. You now have two players on the left and right wide areas. These players know what it takes to attack and defend and have great chemistry with each other.

4-1-3-2 system (positive)

The key to this system is the holding midfield player. The holding midfield position is there to disrupt the opposition's attack and maintain possession while offering support in front of the defensive line and behind the attacking midfielder and attackers. The defensive central midfielder should be able to read the phases of play effectively and have good awareness of passing options, and they must be disciplined in maintaining and organizing shape, balance, and depth to their team. This position has become standard in today's modern game. The holding midfield role is just as important as a goalkeeper. Coaches will not play without one (or two).

In today's game, there is a lot of responsibility on the striker. The majority of teams only play with one striker. This makes it so easy for the two opposing central defenders. I like to play with two quick forwards who relish 1v1 situations. Center backs hate this. The system below shows the player on the ball having many passing options. This is especially important at the youth level. Teaching your players to help the man on the ball is crucial.

The right back receives the ball and has a number of options for passing. The right back chooses the pass depending on the defensive position of the opposition. They also have the option to hit the long pass if all options shown are covered by the defending team.

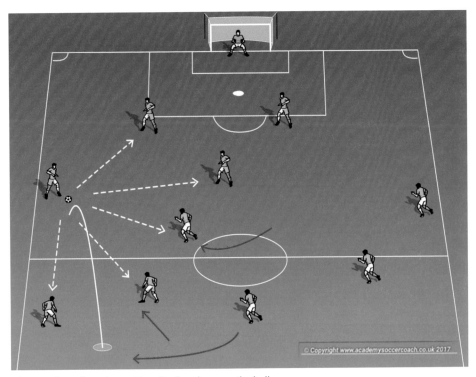

There are lots of passing options for the player on the ball.

1-4-1-3-2 system (negative)

A possible drawback to playing in this system is when you come up against three players in the central playing area. Even professional teams struggle against an effective three-player midfield. If you want to keep playing the same system throughout the game, then your players have to know how to accommodate the extra midfielder. One of the central defenders can step up and guard an attacking opposition midfielder, or one of the strikers can drop in and guard the opposition's holding midfielder.

Many strikers are not disciplined enough to do this effectively, so you may need to substitute one of your two strikers.

The system is rigid. That rigidity is caused by the 4-4-2 fomration's three lines of players which can allow opposing players to find pockets of space between the lines, especially between the defense and the midfield. A well-disciplined team will compress the space between the defense and midfield so as to avoid this, but a poorly organized 4-4-2 can leave huge amounts of space in front of the defense and, if the midfield cannot close down the passing lanes, teams can be ripped apart by opposition players lurking in those

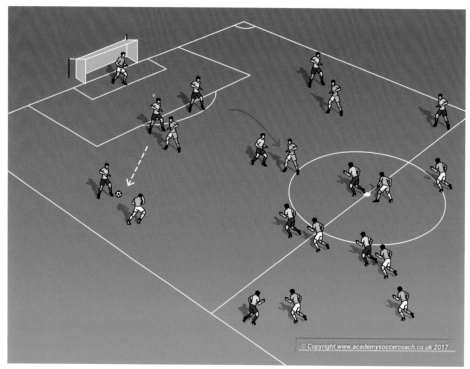

The striker drops back to guard the opposition's holding midfield player.

spaces. It is also hard to play with a 10. If you are up against a midfield three and your team is struggling to cope, you could sacrifice a striker and change the system to a 1-4-2-3-1.

1-4-3-3 formation

If the team plays 4-3-3, then the coach decides if they want one or two holding midfield players. Both fullbacks are encouraged to move forward when attacking. The holding midfield players will be offering good cover for the fullbacks and the wide players. The holding midfielders are the pivotal point when playing this system. They must be capable of disrupting the opposition's attack and maintaining possession for their team. They offer support in front of the defensive line and support behind the attacking midfielder and forwards. The defensive central midfielder should be able to read the phases of play effectively and have good awareness of passing options; they must also be disciplined in maintaining and organizing shape, balance, and depth for their team. This player will be the eyes and ears of the coach and is commonly given the captain's role.

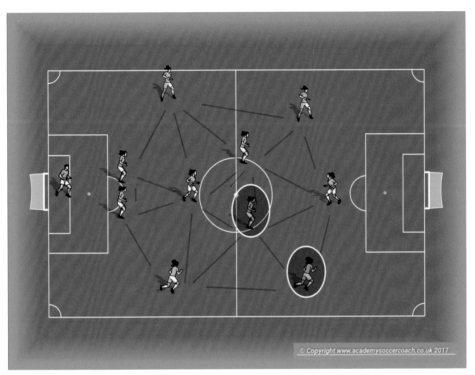

Two players are added in these areas when you move to 11v11.

When possession is lost, the 1-4-3-3 formation almost becomes a 1-4-5-1 system as the two wide players should drop back into the middle third to compact the opposition's midfielders. The wide players must understand when to drop back and defend and when to stay high and ready for an attack. If the opposition is playing a 4–4–2 system, there is also the opportunity to press for the ball higher up the pitch in the attacking third. This can force the opposition to play more directly through to their forwards and allow more chances to regain possession. The system also allows for quality counterattacks. As soon as possession is gained, the team must be prepared to create width, depth, and support at pace, and can sometimes be seen as a counterattacking tactic against strong teams. When possession is won, you will have players in good positions that are ready to attack.

4-3-3 system (positive)

The 4-3-3 is the most popular of all modern formations. There's a reason why many of the most dominant sides of European soccer use it. The game enjoys a player who can play the 10 role. The system creates lots of triangles on the pitch and allows your fullbacks to attack a lot.

The 4-3-3 works great when pressing the opposition.

In possession, the 4-3-3 allows at least seven players to attack, as the wide forwards squeeze the defense, the fullbacks come up behind them, and two of the central midfielders push forward.

However, the special quality of a good 4-3-3 is the pressing quality it brings when possession is lost. This comes from combining two elements: a three-man central midfield which can dominate possession via passing triangles and three strikers who can press high up the pitch (see below). Opponents find it hard to get the ball and even harder to keep it. Midfielders can't get hold of the ball and are pressured quickly when they do. The defenders are faced with three men pressing them, and there are no easy balls to the wings when the fullbacks push up.

4-3-3 system (negative)

If the coach encourages both fullbacks to move forward, then two holding midfielders may work better. One potential drawback of having three attackers occurs when the ball is switched to the wide players; the central player can become isolated in and around the penalty area when the cross is delivered. In this scenario, it is imperative that the opposite winger joins the central striker in the danger areas along with at least one of the two attacking midfielders. At

The wide attacker has moved into the middle to get behind the defenders. The fullback has moved forward to occupy the wide position in case the team needs to switch the play.

the same time, the other attacking central midfielder will look for pullbacks and knockdowns a little deeper than the first attacking midfielder. When one wide player has the ball, the opposite wide player should move more centrally. When they do this, the fullback on their side stays wide so that if the team needs to switch play, they can (see below).

The two forward wide players need to be lively and provide width in attack and defensive support when not in possession. The two wide attacking forwards should like to run or dribble with the ball, but they should also be comfortable dropping back to support the defensive line when needed. The wide position in this 4-3-3 formation can be a physically demanding role and demands a quality end product.

The lone forward can play several roles in this system depending on their strengths as an individual and the tactics and weaknesses of the opposing back line. Some use the striker as a battering ram to create depth to the side, making their runs between the two center backs and keeping these two players occupied. This creates space for the two wingers to attack the fullbacks in 1v1 situations. Using this battering ram creates an immediate outlet when possession is regained and suits a strong, robust striker.

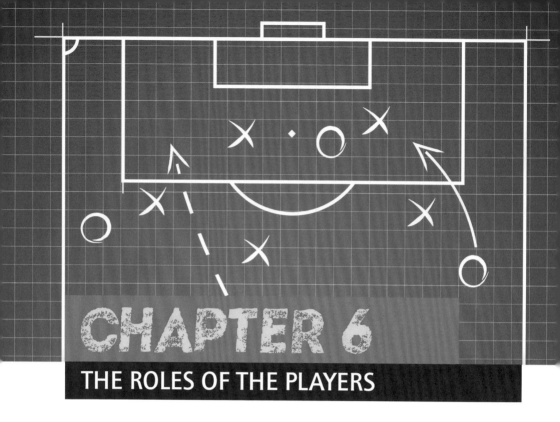

CHAPTER 6
THE ROLES OF THE PLAYERS

THE GOALKEEPER

Attack

- Focus on accurate distribution.
- Is the opposition out of balance to start a quick attack?
- Look for the dangers before you execute the throw or kick.
- Good decision making is important.
- Always be in a position to receive a back pass.
- Get in a good position when your team is in the opposition half. Do not switch off.

Defense

- Be aware of your positioning.
- Organize your team and look for dangers that could occur.

- Decide when to catch, deflect, or punch the ball.

- Communicate clearly to your teammates (e.g., "Keepers!" "Time!" "Away!" "Get goal side!" or "Man on!")

Set pieces

On defense

- Organize your wall quickly and clearly.

- Try to get into a position where you have a good view of the ball.

- Be ready to react to a shot or a ball coming in behind the defense.

Set pieces

On attack

- Stay focused and make sure the guys on defense are not day dreaming.

Corners

On defense

- Help to organize your defense.

- Be ready to catch or punch the ball at the highest point possible.

- Call out "KEEPERS!" or "AWAY!"

- Get your defense to push out when the ball is safe.

- Place suitable defenders on each post.

On attack

- Position yourself on the edge of your penalty area and stay focused.

- Make sure the players on defense are focused.

Technical

- Have excellent handling skills and throws.

- Know when to catch, parry, or deflect.

- Have the ability to control and pass the ball with both feet over a variety of distances.

- Be confident in dealing with crosses even when the area is congested.

Tactical

- Have a good starting position when in or out of possession.

- Understand the tactics of the team and communicate effectively. Distribute the ball more often by throwing it to a teammate rather than punting it (see figure).

- Know when to communicate. Do not just speak for the sake of speaking. Your defense will tune you out if you are just calling out things that are not related to what is happening on the field.

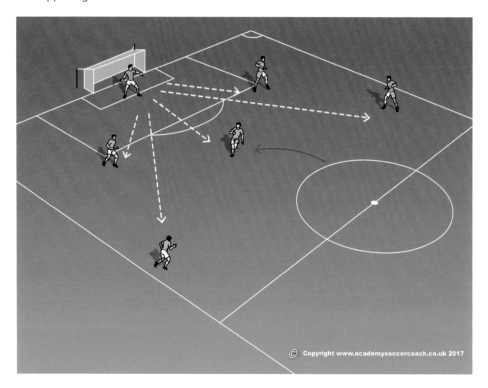

- Initiate the attack and know when the opposition is out of balance.
- Never go up for set pieces, even in the final minute.

Physical

- Have the flexibility, agility, and athleticism to move around the goal with speed, balance, and coordination.
- React quickly in thought and in movement.
- Have the strength to deal with physical contact.

Psychological

- Be capable of staying focused after making a mistake that leads to a goal. Losing focus and berating yourself or teammates after a mistake provides no feedback and could possibly cause another mistake. Learn to move forward and not dwell in the past. Be determined to stop or catch the next shot or cross. Take pride in keeping a shot out.
- Be brave and confident when organizing your defense.
- Have the courage to dive at the opponent's feet.
- Be positive and play with presence.

THE CENTER BACK

Attack

- Be prepared to receive the ball from the goalkeeper.
- Know when to run with the ball and when to pass to a teammate.
- Get in a position behind the attack for support.
- Be available for back passes.
- Be patient. Once you pass the ball, offer support for a possible return pass.
- Switch the point of attack.
- Make diagonal passes behind the opposition's wide midfielders or fullbacks.

Defense

- Maintain a good position.

- Communicate with fellow defenders and the midfielders in front of you.

- Anticipate passes.

- React to the second ball.

- Win your 1v1 battle.

- In 1v1 situations, do not lunge in. Think about the timing of the tackle.

- Try to prevent shots at goal.

- Understand when to mark tight and when to mark loose.

- If the opposition is in balance and your goalkeeper has the ball, make sure you cover the middle area.

Set piece

On defense

- Mark your man or zone.

- Stand in the wall if required.

- Be competitive.

- React to the second ball.

On attack

- Take the free kicks from the defensive third.

- Get in support for free kicks in the middle third.

- Go up for kicks in the attacking third, or stay back and be one of the defenders.

Corners

On defense

- Mark your man or zone.

- Attack the ball at the highest point.

- Block runs from the attackers.

- Put pressure on the second ball.

- Communicate to teammates.

- Clear the lines and push out on the keeper's call.

On attack

- Move up and enter the opposition's penalty area.

- Make runs to score or to screen opposition defenders.

- Get back quickly when the attack breaks down.

Technical

- Be capable of heading the ball well.

- Run with the ball into midfield and beyond.

- Pass the ball with both feet with accuracy and over a variety of distances.

- Take a good defensive stance when defending.

Tactical

- Understand when to mark tight and when to mark loose. Read the game well according to game circumstances (see picture).

- Understand pressure, delay, cover, and balance.

- Cover other defenders and guard space effectively.

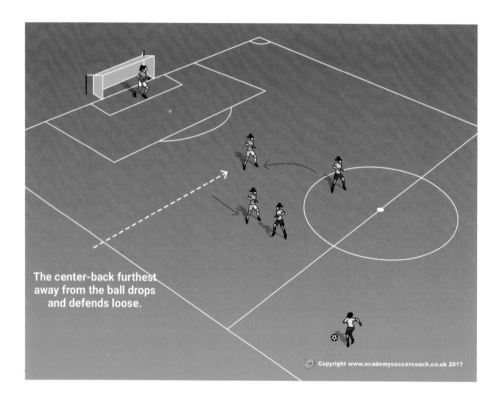

The center-back furthest away from the ball drops and defends loose.

- Track players' movements and communicate when passing an opposition player onto teammates.

- Communicate tactics to others. Make sure the midfielders are doing their jobs.

Physical

- Relish the 1v1 competition.

- Be quick over short distances.

- Have the strength to deal with physical contact.

- Compete aerially with good spring and timing, and be strong in the tackle.

Psychological

- Be capable of regaining focus after a mistake.
- Be brave and focused throughout the game.
- Be a good leader.
- Be competitive.
- Take pride in keeping a shot out.

The center back farthest away from the ball will drop and defend loose.

THE FULLBACK

Attack

- Be prepared to receive the ball from the goalkeeper.
- Decide when to pass, when to run with the ball, when to cross, and when to shoot.
- Communicate, calling for the ball.
- Be a key player when it comes to attacking.
- Anticipate when the ball can be switched to your side of the field.
- Take all throw-ins on your side of the field.
- Be ready to act as the third man running for a pass.
- Overlap and cross.

Defense

- Support the wide midfield player and the center backs.
- Make good recovery runs.
- Win your 1v1 battle against the opposing wide player.
- Force the play away from goal.

- Try not to dive into tackles.

- Make the tackle when you are balanced and ready.

- When the ball is won, start an attack.

- Make the right decision when you clear the ball.

Set pieces

On defense

- If the coach wants you in the wall, be in the wall.?

- Mark your man or zone.

On attack

- Offer support if you are not taking the free kick.

- Look to offer cover if too many players move forward.

- Be prepared to sacrifice going forward for the good of the team.

- Be ready to switch the ball if possible.

Corners

On defense

- Be ready to be on post if the coach so desires.

- Mark a zone or a player.

- Communicate to teammates.

- Attack the ball; do not let it bounce.

- Be able to clear the ball to a teammate.

On attack

- Be able to cause a problem on a corner.
- Take a position outside the penalty area.
- Be prepared to get back quickly.

Technical

- Be capable of heading the ball well.
- Run with the ball and have quality ball control when receiving the ball on the back foot.
- Have great vision.
- Cross the ball with quality.

Tactical

- Understand you are a right- or left-sided player and always be ready to start an attack. Attack and defend (see figure).
- Understand when to mark tight and when to mark loose. Read the game well according to game circumstances.
- Understand pressure, delay, cover, and balance.
- Cover other defenders or midfielders and guard space effectively.
- Track players' movements and communicate when passing an opposing player onto teammates.

Physical

- Relish the 1v1 competition.
- Have a fantastic fitness level. Be quick over long distances.

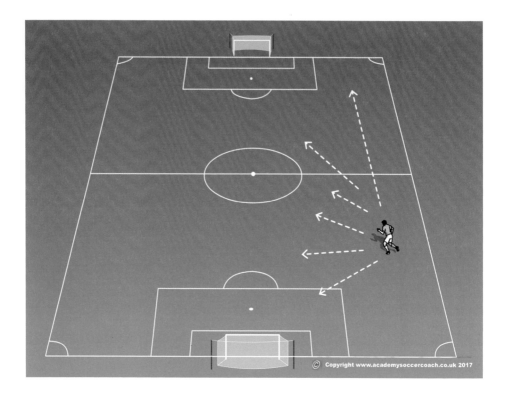

- Have the strength to deal with physical contact.
- Compete aerially with good spring and timing.
- Be strong in the tackle.

Psychological

- Be capable of regaining focus after a mistake.
- Be brave and focused throughout the game.
- Maintain a positive approach to defending and attacking.
- Be competitive.
- Communicate often with wide midfielder and forward.

THE DEFENSIVE MIDFIELDER

Attack

- Support! Support! Support! Create space to receive the ball.

- Be reliable in possession with an excellent first touch and ball control.

- React when the ball is won. Use awareness and vision to work out attacking options.

- Be comfortable passing short or long into space or to feet.

- Make late runs to create scoring opportunities.

- Be proficient in long-distance shooting.

- Run with the ball.

- Move forward or pass forward when possible.

Defense

- Protect the back line.

- Communicate with the midfield and forward and make sure the correct players are returning on defense.

- Delay the play so your teammates can recover.

- Understand when to apply pressure on the ball.

- Win your 1v1 challenges, and react to the loose ball.

- React when the ball is lost by making a tackle or recovering to a good defensive position.

- Man-mark players when required.

- Anticipate and intercept passes through midfield.

Set pieces

On defense

- Prevent quick free kicks.

- Take up a position in the wall if required.

- Communicate to your teammates and look to make sure all players are guarded properly.

- React to the second ball.

- Challenge for the ball.

On attack

- Take free kicks in the middle and attacking thirds.

- Provide support and cover.

- Look for potential dangers if the ball is lost

Corners
On defense

- Play to your strengths.

- Look to see where your forwards are so you can quickly start an attack.

- Communicate with your teammates.

On attack

- Patrol the edge of the penalty area and attack cleared balls.

- Go and receive the ball from the corner taker.

- Make late runs into the penalty area.

- Check your defense to see if they have organized properly.

- Stay back and let the center backs go up.

Technical

- Have the ability to receive the ball and protect it.

- Have quality ball control and the ability to pass over a variety of distances.

- Be able to shoot from distance.

- Be a good one-touch passer.

- Play with an open body stance.

- Do not play predictably; play with disguise.

Tactical

- Have excellent soccer knowledge of the position and your teammates.

- Spot dangers and opportunities quickly.

- See ahead of the present situation.

- Protect the back line on defense and the forward line on offense (see figure).

- Communicate with every team member positively and clearly.

- Always look for weaknesses in the opposition.

- Understand game management.

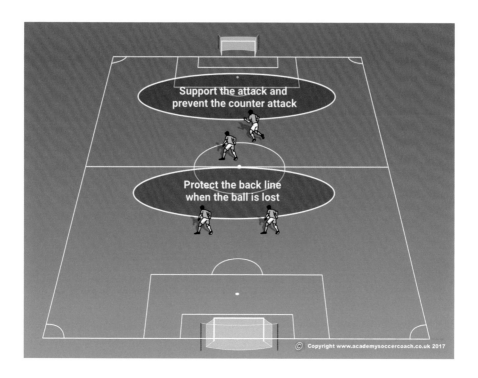

Physical

- Have a high fitness level.
- Be quick over short distances.
- Be a good tackler and header of the ball.
- Love competition.

Psychological

- Adapt your playing style according to the game.
- Be unselfish and understand *TEAM*.
- Have an inner self-belief.
- Have a controlled and positive competitive attitude.

THE ATTACKING MIDFIELDER

Attack

- Create space to either receive the ball or for teammates to exploit.
- Have the ability to turn and dribble.
- Support the forwards.
- Time runs carefully. You may be the third man running.
- Link up play between defense and attack.
- Have the forethought to play in tight areas.
- Think ahead. Have the vision to see the next few options.
- Look to get behind the opposition's defense and beat the offside trap.

Defense

- React to lost possession and make good recovery runs.
- Do not switch off.

- Work for the team.

- Put pressure on the ball if you are the closest player to it.

- Be ready to cover for fullbacks when possession is lost.

- Encourage the forwards to defend from the front and offer cover behind them.

- Keep thinking ahead. Win the ball and counterattack if possible.

Set pieces

On defense

- Take up a position in the wall if required.

- Guard an opponent.

- Challenge for the ball and prevent shots.

- Win the loose ball and push out. Attack at speed if possible.

On attack

- Take direct free kicks in the attacking third if allowed; be creative.

- Make clever movement off the ball.

- React first to the loose ball.

Corners

On defense

- Communicate with your teammates.

- Get ready to start an attack. Be aware of where the forwards are located.

- Man-mark or mark space as necessary.

- Look around to see if everyone is doing their job defensively.

On attack

- You may take the corner; be creative.
- Move around the penalty area in an attempt to to lose your defender.
- Attack the ball.
- React first to the loose ball.
- Follow up any shot from a teammate.

Technical

- Have the ability to receive the ball, run with it, and protect it.
- Have quality ball control and passing.
- Be a good finisher.
- Be a good one-touch passer.
- Do not play predictably; play with disguise.

Tactical

- Have excellent soccer knowledge of the position and your teammates; know you have to defend.
- Spot dangers and opportunities quickly. Know when to press.
- See ahead of the present situation.
- Move anywhere on the field and be very creative in your movement (see figure).
- Communicate and support teammates.
- Always look for weaknesses in the opposition's defense. Look to break the offside.
- Understand game management and know when to sit in and when to play defensively.

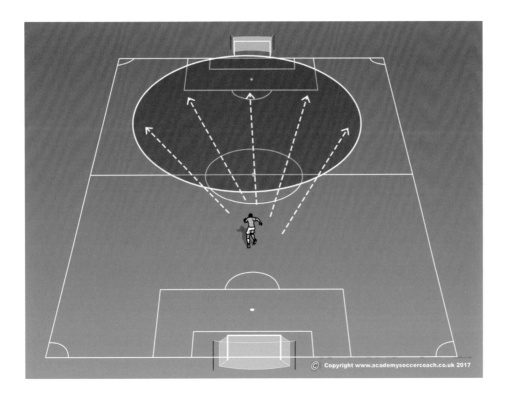

Physical

- Be quick over short and long distances.

- Be a good tackler and header of the ball.

- Love competition.

- Have amazing stamina and be able to last a whole game.

Psychological

- Adapt your playing style according to the game.

- Wear down the opposition.

- Have an inner self-belief.

- Have a controlled and positive competitive attitude.

THE WIDE MIDFIELDER
Attack

- Keep the width, and stay wide.

- The first opportunity you get, dribble against the opposition to see how good they are at defending in a 1v1 situation.

- If they are really good, then play a give and go to get by them.

- Lift your head up to see what options you have. Deliver effective crosses.

- Use quality close control and dribbling skills.

- Try to make runs behind the defensive line. Move more centrally when the ball is on the opposite wing.

- When the ball is on the opposite wing, make diagonal runs.

Defense

- Work with the forward to either delay or pressure opponents in the attacking third.

- Make recovery runs to help the defense when needed.

- Communicate with your teammates.

- Understand when to mark tight and when to mark loose.

- Be aggressive and win the ball back.

- If you are in a 1v1 race for the ball, block the opponent's run while running for the ball.

- Do not let the opposition attacker stand by your side. Keep them in your sight and defend goal side.

Set pieces

On defense

- Be prepared to be in the wall or to defend wide areas.

- Mark a player or a space.

- Stay focused and mark goal side.
- Win the loose ball and attack.

On attack

- You may take the kicks from wide areas or in the attacking third.
- Combine with a teammate to take an indirect free kick.
- Make angled runs behind the defensive line.

Corners

On defense

- You may guard front or back post.
- You may stay upfield and, if so, be ready to counterattack.
- When the ball is won, break at speed.

On attack

- Take the corner.
- Be involved in a short corner.
- Make attacking runs.
- Take up a position on the edge of the penalty area.

Technical

- Have excellent ball control and speed.
- Beat an opponent 1v1.
- Have quality passing and crossing while on the move.
- Score goals.
- Have good aerial ability.
- Be very creative.

Tactical

- Always how for the ball and understand that your movement can take you to the opposite side of the field (see figure).

- Always look for weaknesses in the opposition's defense.

- Elude tight marking.

- Know you have a role to play when defending and be in constant communication with the fullback.

- Make great decisions.

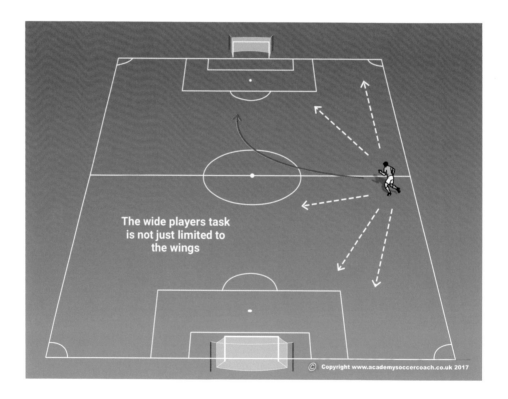

The wide players task is not just limited to the wings

Copyright www.academysoccercoach.co.uk 2017

Physical

- Have an explosive pace in and out of possession.

- Enjoy the 1v1 challenge with the opposition fullback.

- Have great endurance to last a whole game.

- Be agile.

Psychological

- Sometimes be selfish but also be quick to accept responsibility.

- Maintain a positive approach in attack.

- Shrug off mistakes and get back to being focused on the task.

- Be a humble game-changer.

THE FORWARD

Attack

- Maintain a position close to the last defender.

- Don't be easy to mark; keep busy.

- Be capable of holding up the ball and waiting for support.

- Use quick one touch passing when needed.

- Accurately time runs.

- Work out the opposition's weaknesses on defense.

- Create chances for others.

- Be aware of your surroundings.

Defense

- React to lost possession in the attacking third.

- Press quickly to win the ball back.

- Stay focused when the ball is lost.

- Keep moving into positions that enable your teammates to get you the ball once possession is won.

- Mark the opposition's holding midfield player.

SET PIECES

On defense

- Stay upfield and get ready to receive the ball when possession is won.

- Defend the opposition's back line.

- If you are dominant in the air, go back and help the defense.

On attack

- Take the penalty kicks.

- Combine with a teammate for indirect free kicks.

- Be strong in the air when free kicks are taken from wide areas.

- Have quick and late movement.

CORNERS

On defense

- Go back and defend if your height and heading ability is good; if not, stay up.

- If you stay up, stand between the marking defenders.

- Be focused for the clearance.

On attack

- Be the main target.

- Move to get away from defenders.

- Take a gamble on your movement.

- Be good at one-touch finishing.

- React to the loose ball.

Technical

- Have good ball control and be ready to react to any incoming pass.

- Link up with teammates with quality passing.

- Protect the ball well.

- Have great shooting technique.

- Be quick on the turn and effective in 1v1 situations.

Tactical

- Understand how to position yourself in and out of possession.

- Create movement to frustrate the opposition.

- Have the ability and awareness to exploit the space behind the back line.

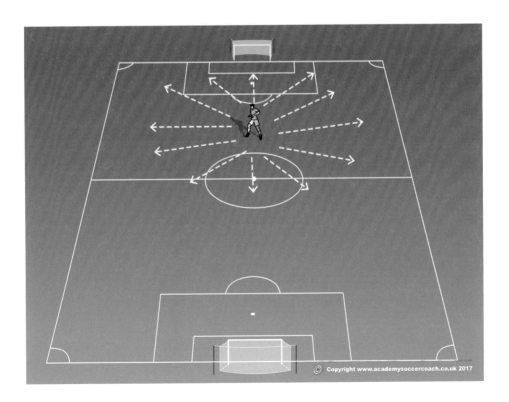

- Escape being marked with timely and intelligent movement.

- Be prepared to sacrifice yourself for the good of the team by making the opposition defend poorly so other teammates can attack.

- Defend from the front; prepare the trigger player for the press.

Physical

- Have explosive speed over short distances.

- Be willing to work just as hard when the ball is lost.

- Have good body strength, spring, and timing for heading the ball.

- Love the challenge against the opposition defenders.

Psychological

- Be mentally strong. If you miss an opportunity, you have to bounce back and think "I'll get the next one!"

- If the opposition defender is getting the better of you, keep working hard and figure out different ways to be successful. Enjoy this challenge.

- Show bravery in goal-scoring situations.

- Be competitive and composed.

CONCLUSION

I find so much fulfillment in helping coaches and players. I have a real passion for developing myself and others. I also find fulfillment in donating to charity through soccer. You have to find fulfillment in your coaching. You have to understand why you are teaching soccer to the athletes. When you have a clear sense of *why* you coach, you will be able to make better decisions that affect the development of your players. I have seen it too many times. When a coach has the wrong "why," the team barely progresses, and five years down the road, you are looking at a player and a team that has very little soccer knowledge. I believe the main character a coach needs is authenticity. An athlete craves authenticity. They want a relationship with someone who cares.

You have to show the team that you are the hardest worker, that you care, and that your coaching philosophy works. If there is no authenticity and love, then there will be no coaching. One of the most powerful indications of caring is hard work. Players will feed off their coach's work ethic. Sometimes coaches see authenticity and caring as a weakness. I believe it is a strength.

If you have the authenticity, then you will make connections with your players and other coaches in your club. Once connections are made, you can then pull together and work on a development plan. Every youth coach that joins a team or club should be open minded to a development philosophy. They must always think of the bigger picture. The end point is development, and the basis for the strict system of play is game intelligence. The coaches and players know from the start exactly how the finished product should look. When players move to 11v11, they will have the knowledge to execute any system of play.

Everyone involved needs to be well informed and pulling in the same direction. Communication with parents and coaching staff is so important. The coaching staff must always be welcoming when a parent wants to talk about their child. When you are working off a development plan, you become more comfortable speaking the truth. The parent may not always like what they hear, but because you are following a process, your response to questions and concerns will be consistent. Parents must be kept well informed of what is happening, otherwise the athlete may find themselves listening to two different versions of the same story. It goes without saying that players will always lean toward the more favorable version, and this is usually bad for their development. You want the parent to buy into the culture of learning so they, too, can educate the player about standards and behavior.

WINNING V'S PLAYER DEVELOPMENT

The most important thing in sports is to take part and play. The culture of winning in children's sports causes damage on a daily basis, not just to children, but also to the clubs where they play.

Winning is important—*FOR THE PLAYER!* At youth development, winning should not be the motivation of the parent or the coach. From a player's perspective, it's all about winning. If they are not winning, the coach has to come up with a plan that gets the group believing they are on the right track. If the coach does not have a philosophy or plan, the players will not believe in the bigger picture.

Here in the US, they have more dropouts from the game than in any other country because its structure is not about player development, it's about winning. How can you build a successful soccer program if your training program is determined by the fact that clubs stop at nothing to win? I coached at one club whose definition of success was based on how many state cups they won. They were not at all concerned that the dropout rate for members was really high.

Instead of having the play-to-win mentality, the leaders of any soccer club should have the philosophy that we play to learn. As parents, we play a huge part in positioning our children in an environment where we feel they can learn and develop. Soccer is a virtual classroom. Would we allow our schools to teach the same way our soccer clubs do? Would we allow our school teachers to walk into the classroom and teach whatever they want?

There are two different paths to take when developing a soccer player or team:

1. Lead the team to victory in the short term, no matter the cost.

2. Gradually introduce your players to the understanding of what it takes to develop as a soccer player and have a long-term goal.

If the coach or club is only interested in winning, then player development suffers from the following disadvantages:

- The player's size and strength will be a deciding factor for joining a team or winning a game.

- The late bloomers will never get the opportunity to bloom.

- Instead of coaching decision makers and becoming a teacher, the coach will play boot ball soccer to accommodate the athletic players. These will be the only tactics, and the majority will be negative and defensive.

The best youth coach is not the one who holds a great win-loss record, but the one who accomplishes a few things:

- They talk about the big picture. They keep their players engaged so that they show up at every practice ready to play and work hard.

- They instill passion and inspire the players to work on their skills away from the practice field.

- They have the skills to run game-related practice sessions to suit the needs of their players. The practice sessions include technical, tactical, mental, physical, and social aspects.

- The players feel like they are achieving something. They are rewarded because of their efforts.

- They are great communicators. They have no agenda and nothing to hide. They follow a plan.

We all coach players that have various skills, but we have to try and get the best out of all of them. We have no idea who is going to blossom under our leadership. Planning your practice sessions is critical for the development of your players and you as a coach. The modern-day coach has an inner self-belief that they can teach the game correctly and get results. This takes bravery, dedication, and studying. A head coach is not selfish; they are also students of the game.

There is a huge need to educate coaches and parents on a new, more holistic, and game-intelligent approach to developing young soccer players. The most important human muscle has been forgotten about completely—the brain! In the future, we have to consider soccer to be a game of knowledge—a cognitive game instead of a physical one! It is about creating decision makers.

There may be unique pressures in soccer (especially in the US) as many parents see sports scholarships as a ticket to future success and as a way of saving vast sums of money on college fees. There can also be an overemphasis on athleticism and strength.

In the modern game of soccer, these talents have become less important, being replaced by greater skills and game intelligence. It is critical to consider the brain as the greatest power on the soccer field. Give me an ounce of intelligence over a pound of muscle any day!

If the natural competitiveness, athleticism, and creativity of kids were harnessed in a more optimal development model, then we would truly keep more players involved and get the opportunity to see the late bloomers bloom.

I spent three years at Foothills SC in Oregon. I purposely joined the soccer club so that I could implement the philosophy in this book. The system works! We started with four teams and three coaches. In three years, we had 22 teams with 17 coaches. We had some success on the field, and the players and parents in the community seemed to enjoy what the soccer club was offering. We had coaching staff that were open-minded when it came to following a development plan. The success was seeing the players develop and become part of a team. Our definition of success was completely different than many other clubs. Players at Foothills SC developed their soccer knowledge while thriving in an environment that was structured. I also had some coaching staff that did not follow the plan. It was evident who was on board and who was not. I'm sure many can relate to the following table, especially the right column.

Followed the plan	Ignored the plan
The team progressed up the divisional ladder.	The team stayed in the same division. If there was movement, it was down.
The team did not win every game, but they did have a purpose in their play.	The group had no understanding of the game. No player rotations, no overlaps, no laying the ball back and no defensive cover.
On game day, you could see they understood teamwork.	
96% of the players stayed in the group.	A turnover in players each year.
Good communication from numerous teammates.	No leadership skills.
Players were very rarely late for practice or games.	Coach and players would be unprepared and lots of players would be late.
Great communication.	Poor communication.
Happy parents and players.	Poor player body language and disgruntled parents.

You can read this book over and over, but the ability to act at the right moment—to make an accurate analysis and to show how things should be done—is much more important.

Understanding your players and their strengths comes with experience. Learning from your mistakes is crucial in your development.

I encourage you to show this book to board members and technical directors of your club. If you get the right people involved and follow a process, you cannot fail.

If you would like to implement this system into your soccer club, please reach out to me. I would love to help. Go to www.soccerpracticesessions.com where you can find practice sessions related to the age group that you are coaching.

Good luck!

ACADEMY SOCCER COACH

Academy soccer coach is a company that provides digital solutions for coaches at all levels of the game. Our coaching software enables coaches, clubs, and professional organizations to plan and prepare their sessions remotely from anywhere in the world.

ASC works with the following professional clubs and organizations:

United Soccer Coaches, US Soccer, Fulham FC, West Ham Utd, Stoke City FC, Newcastle United FC, Portland Timbers, Crystal Palace FC, Sporting Kansas, The Irish FA, The PFA, and many more.

For more information on ASC and the service we provide, please visit www.academysoccercoach.com.

CREDITS

Design and Layout

Cover Design: Annika Naas
Interior Design: Anja Elsen
Layout: Amnet Systems

Illustrations

Cover and Chapter Illustration: © AdobeStock
Interior: © Jason Carney, unless otherwise noted

Editorial

Managing Editor: Elizabeth Evans
Copyeditor: Anne Rumery